Stenciling
the Arts & Crafts Home

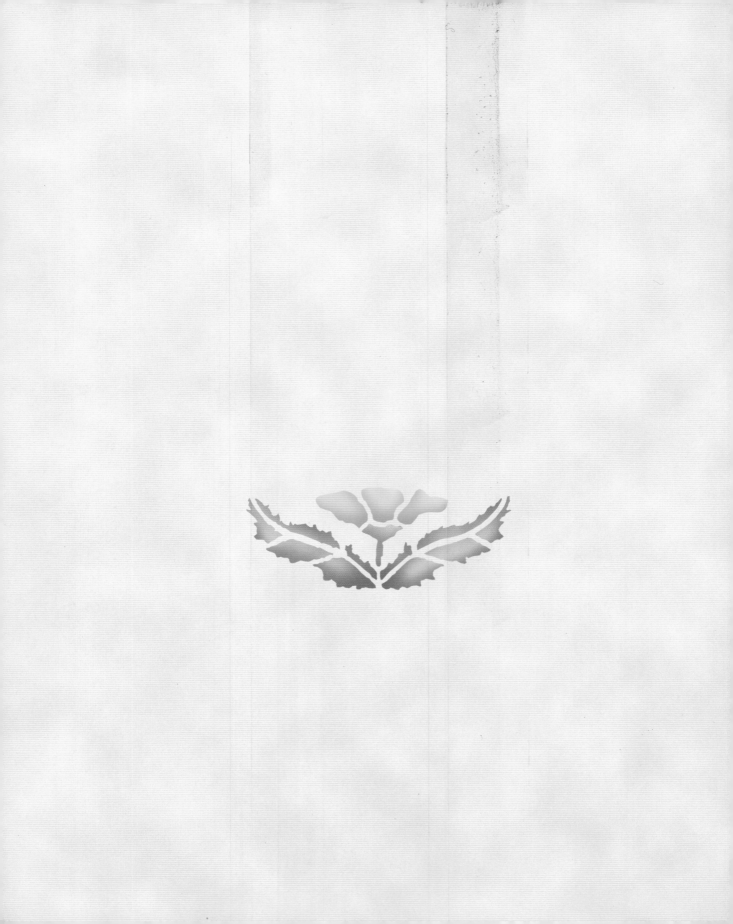

Stenciling
the Arts & Crafts Home

A Comprehensive Guide to Beautifying
Your Bungalow

--- --- --- ---

Amy A. Miller

Gibbs Smith, Publisher
Salt Lake City

First Edition
10 09 08 07 06   5 4 3 2 1

Text © 2006 Amy A. Miller
Photographs © Amy A. Miller, except as follows:
© 2006 Stephen Braker and David Brier: pages 10, 30, 33, 34, 46, 48–50, 52–54,
57–59, 63, 67, 72, 74, 76, 84, 85, 100, 101, 103–112, 114–117, 119, 121.
Linda Svendsen: pages 12, 38 (bottom), 38, 40, 41 (upper and lower left), 42.

Published by
Gibbs Smith, Publisher
P.O. Box 667
Layton, Utah 84041

Orders: 1.800.835.4993
www.gibbs-smith.com

Designed by Maralee Oleson / m:GraphicDesign
Printed in China

Library of Congress Cataloging-in-Publication Data

ISBN 1-58685-439-9
Miller, Amy (Amy A.)
  Stenciling the arts & crafts home : beautifying your bungalow / Amy
Miller.—1st ed.
      p. cm.
  1. Stencil work. 2. Arts and crafts movement. 3. Interior decoration.
I. Title. II. Title: Stenciling the arts and crafts home.

NK8654.M55 2006
745.7'3–dc22

2006010743

For my dear friend, Paul Duchscherer, who not only gave me
the shove I needed to start my business but continues to point
my shoulders in the right direction.

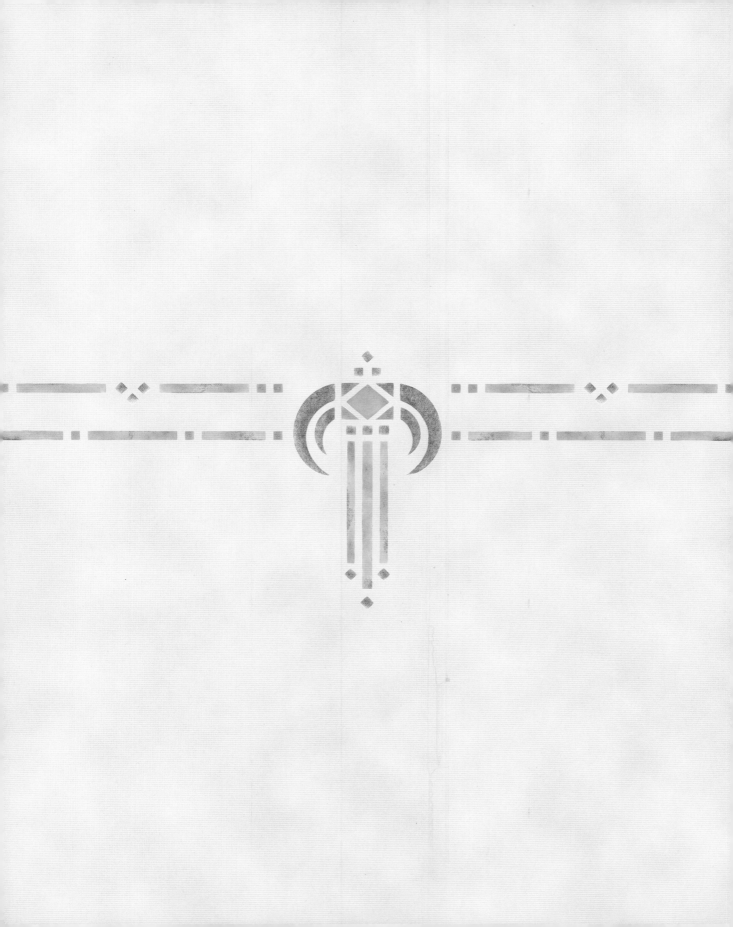

Contents

Introduction

he first thing that seems to come to mind for many people at the mention of the word *stencil* is an image of a little teddy bear with a top hat appearing in some neighbor's bathroom, often applied in some sloppy paint manner with edges smudged and blurred. I have grown to accept those polite face-twisting reactions. Then, I try to explain that stenciling from the Arts and Crafts movement is different and has nothing to do with Popsicle sticks and pom-poms.

Actually, stenciling was a widely used decorative art during that period. Gustav Stickley and others like him encouraged homeowners to participate in the decorative arts of their homes and stenciling was a perfect way to do it. Stenciling was not only applied to walls—the most common area being in the frieze—but was also used to adorn curtains, portieres, pillows and table linens. Stenciled fabrics could then be embellished further with embroidery.

Although embroidered and stenciled linens can still be found, original wall stenciling has mostly disappeared, having been painted over through the years. After all, how many 1915 houses still have original paint on their walls? What's missing are not only the wonderful attempts by a dedicated homeowner, but also the magnificent works of art that some talented professional stenciler applied, likely a journeyman. A typical out-of-sight, out-of-mind situation, wall stenciling from the Arts and Crafts movement has been all but forgotten until now.

Stenciling has become a passion for me. I'm fascinated by the beautiful and unusual techniques that were used in stenciling from this period. When I see original examples, it is like viewing living art. Each example helps me gradually understand how the paints were applied many years ago by a hand such as mine. The simplistic, stylized designs, often focusing on an aspect of nature, are quite varied. There are wonderful designs that are easy to apply and are most likely chosen by the do-it-yourself homeowner. Then there are the fabulous designs that took an expert hand to execute and are reminiscent of Bradbury & Bradbury Art Wallpapers.

I try to document each one that passes my way, but alas, they continue to disappear before I can find them. Still, it pleases me immensely when I walk into an environment and unexpectedly look up to see some hidden little treasure, still radiant even in fading paint, that for some reason still

A typical out-of-sight, out-of-mind situation, wall stenciling from the Arts and Crafts movement has all but been forgotten until now.

exists in its original location like a little jewel forgotten. I am better for viewing it.

So I feel that I must pass it on. A good portion of my time these days is spent educating others on this lost art. I often explain how stenciling was used during this period, or lecture on the various forms and techniques. Sometimes I simply teach others how to stencil. I love watching my classes depart with their little rolled-up samples, their faces beaming at what they have accomplished.

I continue to research, document and relay to others what I have learned about stenciling. My hopes are that this book will not only provide you with the encouragement and desire to try your hand at stenciling, but also help educate you about what uniquely sets this beautiful form of stenciling apart. The old stencils may be passing away as someone new moves in and repaints, but if I have it my way, these beautiful designs from the past will not be forgotten.

- - - Amy A. Miller - - -
Trimbelle River Studio and Design

A History
of Arts & Crafts Stenciling

he art of stenciling can be traced back a long way. There is evidence of stenciling in Egyptian tombs, and as if to echo this ancient art, a stylized form of an Egyptian-style lotus can be found in some of the vintage stenciling catalogs from the early 1900s. Although wall stenciling was rather popular during the Victorian and Early Americana eras, it truly blossomed during the Arts and Crafts period, where it appeared on walls and almost every surface you could think of.

So what makes this stencil book so different from the one I purchased in 1977? Good question. For starters, it doesn't contain any pineapples, geese with bows or a woman in a kitschy little apron ready to stencil a strawberry on a box. Stenciling from the Arts and Crafts movement took a different turn. Yes, there were various forms of fruit and you may uncover a goose (no bow around the neck, though), but none of these motifs would bear much resemblance to their real-life counterpart. Artists from this period used designs that emphasized motifs from nature, but the images took on a stylized form and were more simplistic. Often what turned these simple designs into works of art were the various techniques used to apply them to whatever they adorned.

The Arts and Crafts movement started across the Atlantic Ocean in England toward the end of the 1800s. Men like William Morris, John Ruskin and Charles Rennie Mackintosh pushed their philosophies on hand-crafting and a natural emphasis in living into the public eye as they rebelled against the lack of quality being shown due to mass production. As they succeeded, the movement spread to America. Here, Gustav Stickley, a predominate figure in the progression, began a magazine called *The Craftsman*, which catapulted the Arts and Crafts movement into America's mainstream society. Soon there were furniture makers, potters, coppersmiths and more, all promoting wares created by a craftsmanship that was rapidly disappearing.

As society moved away from the Victorian era, a new form of housing was increasing in popularity. The quaint little bungalow began springing up all over the country as folks moved away from the

Stylized natural motifs and the techniques used in applying the paint made stencils from the Arts & Crafts movement unique.

large Victorian homes known as "Painted Ladies" and the servants required to assist them. The extremely efficient bungalow came equipped with built-in furniture and promoted cozy places to gather; the modern style seemed to assure families it was an easier way to live. You could even order your home through the mail and the train would deliver it to your town! *The Craftsman* was just one of many magazines and catalogs that offered floor plans for bungalows and showed ideas for stenciling.

One of the movement's basic philosophies was to seek peacefulness and pleasure from the natural environment in which we live. Mother Nature influenced home décor with her colors, the natural beauty of unpainted woodwork and honest simple designs reflecting flora and fauna. For the

first time, women were now being encouraged to take part in the decorative arts of their home not only by *The Craftsman* but also by many other women's magazines. Mail-order kits for stencils and linens offering the stylized Arts and Crafts designs appeared everywhere. With the movement's philosophy of returning to nature for inspiration, simplifying one's life and getting away from the Victorian belief of "More is not enough," many believed that following the Arts and Crafts philosophy could actually make one healthier, less stressed and more at peace. Stenciling was an excellent way for homeowners to incorporate this belief into the decorative arts of their households.

At the turn of the nineteenth century, an interesting rumor floated around with regards to the health benefits of painted walls and stenciling. I first heard about the so-called health hazards of wallpaper while listening to a lecture given by Bruce Bradbury, founder of the spectacular Bradbury & Bradbury Art Wallpapers. As I reviewed my numerous vintage stencil catalogs and decorative painting books, I was amazed to see this rumor come to life before my eyes. There may have been some legitimacy back then to the paint companies' claims of dangerous germs hiding out in rotten glue binders used in printing wallpaper, but I'm inclined to believe there was a bit of self-less promoting going on as well. Who wouldn't want to have a cheerful, healthy and cozy home with stenciling and banish that horrible contagious wallpaper! Never mind that the painters used numerous toxic solvents and thinned their lead-based paint with gasoline. Paint and wallpaper have certainly come a long way since then.

Even after considering the supposed health advantages of stenciling, the late-nineteenth-century homeowner could conveniently achieve an exceedingly beautiful and stylish décor. There were splendid lines of stencils available through the ease of mail order, and within weeks, one could incorporate the tranquil effects of nature in pattern and color with stenciling. Imagine how many stencils were sold with that mind-set.

Even outside the germ-free, easy-ordering advantages of stenciling, the desire of the Arts and Crafts movement to incorporate the soothing effects of nature in one's own environment was as popular then as it is today. With our complicated and hectic lifestyles, the hundred-year-old philosophies of the movement are still relevant. At lunch the other day, I opened a fortune cookie to read, "The philosophy of one century becomes the common sense of the next." It is just common sense to me to return to the beauty and tranquility of Arts and Crafts stenciling (and I'm not just attempting to be some shameless promoter).

– – – – –

A Stencil Here and a Stencil There . . .

When people ask me what I do for a living, the answer makes them back off as if I had just said I had leprosy. I have come to understand this reaction. After all, I, too, took part in the resurgence of stenciling in the 1970s and 1980s. Growing up with parents who ran a shop that specialized in "the restoration of antique illuminating devices" for thirty-two years, I was quite familiar with the primitive antiques world and the stenciling of early Americana. I even designed, cut and stenciled my own antiques shop, which eventually led me to the decorative painting field. However, it wasn't until I was hired to stencil a restaurant built in 1917 that I discovered the wonderful and fabulously different world of Arts and Crafts stenciling. So let's get this perfectly clear—when I write about Arts and

– – – – –

It makes common sense to me to return to the beauty and tranquility of Arts and Crafts stenciling.

– – – – –

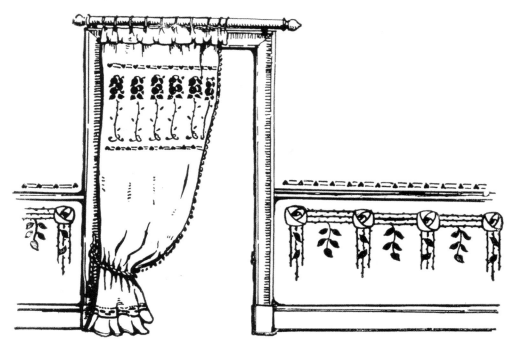

Vintage catalogs offered suggestions for where to use stenciling, such as walls, windows, doors and dado treatments.

Crafts stenciling, I am referring to stenciling from the Arts and Crafts movement; a period of history from about 1900 to about 1925, not stenciled flowerpots at a craft boutique. Now, you could put an Arts and Crafts stencil design on a flowerpot, but that might just be too confusing.

I had no idea when I took that restaurant job just how much stenciling was used during that period. I was familiar with wall stenciling and the occasional immigrant trunk or piece of furniture, but Arts and Crafts stenciling was a whole new world. Stenciling was used everywhere—not just walls, but curtains, portieres, pillows and table linens. Stenciling appeared on all sorts of practical ladies' sundries, from aprons and laundry bags to picture frames and pin cushions. Those who were so inclined could then embellish their stenciled item with various embroidery stitches, using as little or as much as their time or talent allowed. As I said, it was everywhere.

Today, the most common place one thinks of stenciling is still a wall. But even here, Arts and Crafts stenciling took a new approach. Yes, running along the top of the wall close to the ceiling was done, but the Arts and Crafts home, most commonly a bungalow, often had all sorts of wonderful wood moldings to break up the wall and ceiling into perfect palettes for painting. Picture rails created friezes in bedrooms, wood-trimmed panel areas encircled dining and living rooms, and boxed-beam ceilings gave homeowners a variety of areas to stencil. They could follow a crown molding, wainscoting or tile in a bathroom; walls offered numerous options.

But walls were just the beginning. A single motif like a ginkgo leaf or geometric architectural element could be carried throughout the room with a stencil. Table linens, pillows and curtains were excellent areas to continue a theme by creating a simple unity, allowing self-expression in the chosen design and in the personalized color scheme as well.

Stenciling went way beyond walls and linens. In the 1920s, exposed ceiling beams in Spanish- or Mission-influenced dwellings were quite common. A dear friend of mine lives in one of these small Spanish Revival apartment complexes in Los Angeles, originally built for Charlie Chaplin and his crew. Although the walls of her apartment have been painted repeatedly over the years, the rough-hewn beams still bear the colorful rustic stenciling original to the structure.

Womanly items, such as aprons, handbags, laundry bags, and fans, were often stenciled.

A frieze area is stenciled with a peacock design in a billiard room. Notice the curtains and valance are stenciled as well.

One common place for stenciling was along the top of the wall close to the ceiling.

Above: *Wonderful wood moldings broke up the wall and ceiling into perfect palettes for painting. Notice how the stencil was stretched to adapt in the different-sized panels.*

Below: The Craftsman *magazine offered many marvelous options for stenciling, such as using a single Spot stencil repeated in panel areas in the frieze.*

Another rather unusual place Arts and Crafts stenciling can be found is on the exterior of a home. Midwest architects Purcell & Elmslie used exterior stenciling on some of their homes. The Purcell-Cutts home, owned by the Minneapolis Institute of Art, is a charming example of exterior stenciling. The home has original examples of Prairie-style Arts and Crafts stenciling throughout the house, an extra special treat on this delightful home tour.

Discovering the Arts and Crafts Stencil World

When one starts a small business, it is often because one has a passion for something and thinks others will love it too. It is a good conception, with a lot of smiles and grand ideas that grow along the way until one day a little business is born. Oh the joy! How glorious the creation! Then come the "diapers." Just as with a toddler, the small business owner must prepare for the unknown, and those totally unexpected, eye-opening questions that leave them dumbfounded.

My first unbelievable question was repeated often as I debuted my product line: "Can these stencils be used on walls?" Now being a decorative painter, it never occurred to me that anyone would ask such a silly question. After all, didn't everybody know about stenciling? Obviously not. Thankfully I kept my initial reaction to myself and realized I needed to take another approach.

It didn't take long for me to find out just how uneducated the general public was about Arts and Crafts–period stenciling. Thankfully, magazines like *American Bungalow*, *Style 1900* and *Old House Journal* were helping folks understand what painted treasures they had in their beloved little bungalows. Modern-

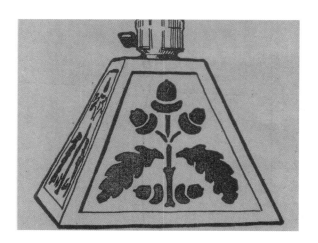

Trunk covers, screen dividers, and even lampshades were other home accessories that could be enhanced with a bit of stenciling.

These original stencils were found under layers of old wallpaper. Notice in the lower photo where washing the wallpaper paste off the wall dissolved the binders in the paint, literally removing it. This is a common problem when discovering old stencils under wallpaper.

This stencil, found under five layers of painted wallpaper, was documented and put back into the room after the walls were repaired.

day craftsmen taught people about the beauty of quartersawn oak and hammered copper. Numerous potters and printers, textile and tile makers all had their place, for these things survived over the years. But how many 1910 houses still bore their original paint? It wasn't just Arts and Crafts wall stenciling that had been lost, but also buried away was the amount of stenciling that had been used on pillows and table runners and curtains throughout these charming abodes.

One day, while talking to my husband about the lack of original stenciling out there, he pointed out that I just didn't know where to look. Suddenly, I understood the mission I had to undertake—where are my red tights and yellow cape when I need them? I would become Super Stencil Hunter and save all the original Arts and Crafts stencils before they were painted over! So I started to dig. The more I dug, the more I learned. I found original period stencils on Masonic Hall ceilings and under layers of wallpaper in old houses. They were indeed out there, but they were rapidly being covered up. I wanted to spend all my time and money in this stencil-recovering adventure, but the task soon became too much for an infant business learning to crawl at a rapid rate and needing a watchful eye. Unless I could clone myself or win the lottery, the tights and cape had to go back into the closet, with only the occasional appearance.

No. 83.
Size 13x12 in.
Price, 80 cents.

No. 84.
Size 16½x11¼ in.
Price, 80 cents.

No. 85.
Size 11½x10½ in.
Price, 80 cents.

Suggestions for pretty pillows: Dutch blue and light blue stenciled on heavy buff silk and outlined with dark blue "mello-tone" rope silk in a simple outline stitch.

A very striking effect may be obtained by stenciling any of the designs shown, in our orange on tan burlap, and outlined with black "mello-tone" rope silk; light blue and leaf green outlined with dark green rope silk to match. This color scheme on cream denim is very dainty.

Although the catalog caption refers to the color scheme as appearing "dainty," these stylized geometric forms of Arts and Crafts stencils give them a somewhat more sophisticated masculine appearance.

What I had discovered along the way was how incredibly unique Arts and Crafts stenciling was. The designs were quite different from the stencil patterns of today. Often working with nature motifs, the simple stylized designs could sometimes be a bit difficult to interpret. I once heard it said that if you found it difficult to decipher what the stencil pattern was actually designed from, it was a true Arts and Crafts design. The Glasgow Rose is a good example of this stylized design; how many square roses have you seen in a garden? Yet this is a widely used motif from the period. The stylized and often geometric form of Arts and Crafts stencils give them a more sophisticated masculine appearance, far from the frilly, scrolling, ribbon-and-bow effects of the Victorian period or the rough and primitive Early American style. Yet Art Nouveau and Art Deco could slip their influences into the design and blend right in with the natural elements of copper, mica, stone and pottery so prevalent in the Arts and Crafts decor.

What also became evident to me were the

- - - - -

I once heard it said that if you found it difficult to decipher what the stencil pattern was actually designed from, it was a true Arts and Crafts design.

- - - - -

various techniques used in the stenciling process. Of course, there were examples of where an Arts and Crafts stencil design had been applied in a solid color or two. Sometimes this provided the desired effect and often was the easiest application method for a novice homeowner, but it was certainly not the only technique. More often, colors were shaded, giving depth to a single color or blended into another completely different hue. This was totally acceptable and even desired. Allowing the colors to blend rather than trying to maintain exact color separation gave the stencil designs an unusual beauty.

stencil and have it delivered directly. Soon, they'd be ready to create the home of their dreams!

Stencils were also manufactured from metals like brass and tin, and were more durable for larger projects. However, they had a more difficult time lying flat against the surface, making stenciling a messier proposition or one better left in the hands of a professional. Flexible canvas was a more unusual material, but it too required treatment with a protective coating to make the flexible fabric less permeable. Overall, the heavy paper stencils would have been the most likely type of stencil

– – – – –

For a mere twenty cents or so, homeowners could purchase a stencil and have it delivered directly. Soon, they'd be ready to create the home of their dreams!

– – – – –

The stencils themselves were made from various materials. The most common was a stiff, heavy paper stock that had been oiled or varnished to protect it. The stock could be purchased uncut (allowing the homeowner to do the work) or precut (saving the homeowner time). Precut mail-order stencils were still mostly cut by hand, but the process was expedited by the use of leatherworking punches. Either way, the stencil would still have to be treated with a protective varnish-like coating. These paper stencils were available through a variety of mail-order catalogs, often distributed by companies that sold paint supplies as well. For a mere twenty cents or so, homeowners could purchase a

that the Arts and Crafts homeowner would have acquired and used.

The most exquisite of all Arts and Crafts stencils was the Outline stencil. Here, only a dashed outline of the design was actually applied in stencil form. Then, using oil-based glazes and a variety of techniques and tools, the stenciler would paint in the design, as if filling in the lines of a coloring book. These stencils were not for a novice but were applied by professional decorative painters at the time. These painters could stay busy enough in a larger town, but if not, they took their art on the road, thus developing the term *journeymen*. Often dining and staying with the folks whose

Vintage color samples show blended colors. A stencil border with matching corners, typical of ceiling and panel work, also shows a decorative background finish that was often used.

Colors were often shaded, giving depth to a single color, or blended into another completely different hue, providing the stencil designs with an unusual beauty.

home they were working on, these artists were traveling salesmen of a different kind. Unfortunately, signatures are rare on original stenciling, and so many of these talented painters may never be known. I often think back to these journeymen when I am out of town on a job of my own, and I'm thankful for the many wonderful friends I have made along this unusual way.

Although I do occasionally run across original stenciling done in water-based paints, more often the oil-based medium was used. Oil-based paint could be just as messy and runny as any water-based, and water-based paint could be mixed into a stiffer consistency. I believe the oil-based medium was used more often because of the way the paint performed. Oil-based paints allowed the artist to work with the paints in a more manipulative way. The shading and blending of colors was much easier to achieve with oil. Better effects, less effort. Isn't that what everyone wants in a task?

The techniques used to apply the paint through the stencil plate varied by the type of

- - - - -

Allowing the colors to blend rather than trying to maintain exact color separation gave the stencil designs an unusual beauty.

- - - - -

Stencil Outfit No. 3.

This outfit is complete in every detail. In addition to twelve 4-inch tubes of stencil colors, it has large tubes of Stencil White and Stencil Medium, three stencil brushes, a stencil cutting knife, one palette knife, a block of thumb tacks, six blank sheets of stencil paper, six ready-cut stencils, one glass palette on which to mix the stencil colors, a book of instructions and a sheet of stencil transfer patterns. This is without doubt the most complete outfit on the market today.

Price $3.00

Sherwin-Williams, among other companies, offered complete kits that could be purchased through mail-order catalogs.

stencil used, the type of paint medium used and the individual painter. Some used the rat-a-tat-tat Woody Woodpecker method of stippling or pouncing, while others preferred more of a swirling method. Either way eventually worked.

Special stencil brushes were the common tool used for the application and today haven't really varied much from a hundred years ago. The brushes back then were made from natural animal hair, usually hog, just like the boar-bristle-quality

Some examples of vintage mail-order catalogs, where homeowners could purchase stencils.

brushes made today. The only exception is that some brushes today are made from cheap synthetic materials like nylon.

Stenciling an Arts and Crafts design today is really similar to stenciling back then. Fortunately, the true differences seen today are for the better. Most stencils are now cut from a material that is far easier to work with and much more durable, and there have been fabulous new products developed to aid the stenciling process. And as for the paints? Amazing improvements. Although I refer to Paintstiks being the consistency of lipstick, I highly recommend you do not use them as such. Otherwise, paints today are much less lethal than their ancestors, and they are much more consistent in application since you do not have to continually thin most of them. In this day and age, I doubt if you'll find any more white lead-based stencil paint and you certainly won't need to thin it with gasoline. I promise you can leave the gas for the car. ■

The Herrick Stencil Book

A Book of Special Designs and Information, Adaptable for Stencilling and Applique

Copyright 1910 and Published by
THE HERRICK DESIGNS COMPANY
246 Michigan Boul.~Chicago.

PRICE, TWENTY-FIVE CENTS

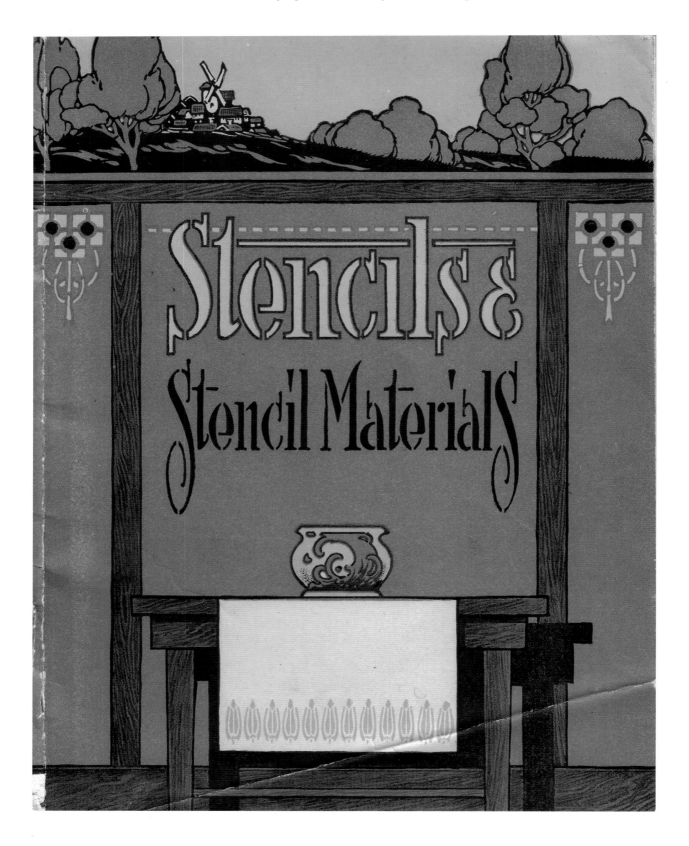

Two vintage mail-order catalogs, originally produced by Sherwin-Williams during the Arts and Crafts movement.

Before You Begin

o, the beauty and simplicity of Arts and Crafts–period stenciling has charmed you and now you want to stencil something. The feeling of invincibility in this new art has taken control and you are ready to run off to the local craft store, stock up on loads of colorful little bottles of acrylic paint and synthetic brushes, and head for the most dominant spot on your living room wall to start your hobby. Whoa, Nellie! Sure it is an easy way to decorate, and part of the beauty of stenciling is that you can just paint over it. But why not have your project come out perfect the first time? The job will be easier and the final outcome will be greatly improved if you learn the advantages of different materials used in stenciling and become aware of your options before you begin. Like everything else in life, the more prepared you are, the easier the task.

A Stencil Is a Stencil Unless It's an Arts and Crafts Stencil

Obviously, the first item you will need to begin stenciling is a stencil. So what exactly is a stencil? A stencil is a pattern or design that is cut out of a material such as plastic or heavy paper stock. When paint is applied on top of the stencil plate, the color is transferred only through the openings, re-creating the design on the chosen surface, such as a wall or a piece of fabric.

Today's modern stencil world is vastly different from what painters would have used a hundred years ago. Originally stencils were hand cut from materials such as heavy-weight paper (referred to as "oil board") or metals such as brass or tin. Stencils these days are most often made out of clear plastic that runs between 5 and 7 millimeters

Facing: *Unpacking and inspecting a 1908 stenciling outfit.*

Above: *Today most stencils are made from flexible plastic rather than heavyweight paper, which was referred to as "oil board."*

thick and are produced in multiples by a computerized laser cutter. I wonder how many modern-day stencil companies realize what a grand invention the laser cutter is to their industry. Besides eliminating the hand-cutting method, another huge advantage these "modern" stencils have over those from yesteryear is that they are transparent, allowing one to see through them. This added benefit aids tremendously in the realignment process. The plastic stencils are also more durable than the varnish-coated, heavy

paper stock and are more flexible than the early metal types.

A good majority of the stencils in the market today consist of multiple overlays or stencil plates, usually to maintain color separation. They can contain as many as ten or more plates for just one design. These multiple stencil plates need to be aligned one on top of another to complete the pattern, as well as stay aligned end over end when used as a border. The end result? Although you may be able to get by with fewer brushes by

This stencil has two overlays. The second overlay is laid on top of the stenciled image produced by the first stencil plate. Alignment is made easy with registration marks.

cleaning and reusing with each different stencil plate, who really wants to go around a room ten times with a ten-overlay stencil? Way too much work! Generally the more stencil plates, the longer the application process will be. Of course, there are times when it is necessary to have more than one stencil plate for a design. For instance, sometimes an extra stencil plate is needed for strength. After all, there can only be so many large holes in a stencil before it becomes floppy. There are times when a separate plate is needed to maintain color separation, as in the stencil pictured above.

Examples of Chain Link stencils, where the same image is basically repeated in succession like the links in a chain.

Arts and Crafts stencils, on the other hand, are more often single overlays, or one stencil plate for one design. Using a separate brush for each color rather than a separate stencil, all the colors used in the design are applied before the stencil plate is moved. This makes the process faster and easier. Occasionally you will find multiple stencil plates used in Arts and Crafts stenciling, but rarely will you find more than two or three plates and often these extra plates are for strength rather than for color separation. A single plate also makes it easier to create the beautiful blending of colors that is so apparent in this period of stenciling.

There are many types of stencil designs in this period of stenciling. Unlike the complicated and often fussy borders from the Victorian period or the simple rustic bits and pieces of designs that were pieced together in early Americana stenciling, this period lent itself to a wide variety of stencil uses and styles. For instance, borders could have consisted of Chain Link, Dominant or Background styles of design. A simple Spot stencil could have been used more sparsely in a frieze area, alone or combined with Beading or as an overall design used like wallpaper. There were very simple designs that the average homeowner could feel comfortable applying to a wall or curtain as well as elaborate Outline stencils that could challenge even a professional painter. So let's start by explaining these styles:

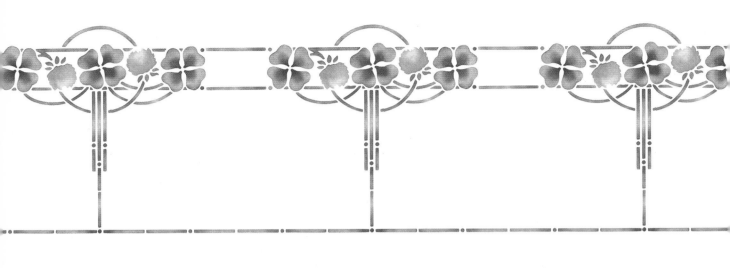

Examples of Dominant stencils, where a dominant image is connected by a less significant image, often a bar pattern.

- Chain Link stencils are stencils that have basically the same image repeated over and over in succession, like the links in a chain. These stencils are some of the most common stencils and often what one might think of as a typical border design.

- Dominant stencils are designs that have a dominant image, like a pendant, connected by a less significant image, often a bar type of pattern. Although one might think that this style would also pertain to modern-day stenciling, its stylized form and distinct layout during the Arts and Crafts period sets it apart from most of what one might call a Dominant stencil.

- Spot stencils are just what they sound like—a spot of design. They were used in a variety of ways, sometimes by themselves, sometimes repeated over and over to form a pattern and sometimes combined with other stencils to form a totally different style of design. Spot stencils were used often in earlier forms of stenciling, especially in early Americana, but again, the uniqueness of the Arts and Crafts designs and the way they were used easily sets this form of spot stenciling apart from others.

- Background stencils are aptly named. Instead of cutting out the design, the background is cut out and stenciled, like a reverse stenciling. Whatever color the wall is underneath the

Example of how a Spot stencil could be used.

stenciled background will be the color of the design. These designs were usually stenciled in just one color, allowing an optical illusion to take place. Sometimes a band of color, the width of the stencil, would be painted on the wall and the background stencil transferred over it. This would then be the color of the design rather than the wall color. Background stencils were usually applied as a running border on a wall, beam or ceiling.

Chain Link, Dominant, Background and Spot stencils were all very common forms of Arts and Crafts–period stenciling that you could run across easily. But there were a few other more unusual styles worth a brief mention.

■ Overall stencils were used like wallpaper, filling an area of a wall or ceiling. They were not nearly as popular as borders and Spot stencils, but still could be found occasionally among Arts and Crafts–period stencils. A single design could be cut like a Spot stencil and repeated numerously or the stencil could be cut as a chunk of design that fitted together like a puzzle when placed side by side and end to end. Considering the amount of work required to lay out this type of design, wallpaper became a time-saving alternative.

■ Relief stencils were created when a design was actually applied in a raised form by using stencils cut from thicker materials like cork or thin slices of soft woods like basswood. The stencil was then filled in with a plaster composition like plaster of paris. Although these raised stencils could be embellished further with stenciled color, the beauty of a simple design with the play of light and shadow was

Outline example, stippled and wiped out.

Instead of cutting out the design, the background of the design is cut out and stenciled. Whatever color the wall is underneath, the stenciled background will be the color of the design. Here the design is applied in iridescent gold on a darker wall.

often enough to give great merit to these unusual stencils.

■ The elegant Outline stencil was perhaps the grandest of all. The stencil, an outline of the design, could be applied in a light, soft color and left as is. More often, it was applied in a dark brown or green and the remaining area filled in freehand, similar in some ways to a child's coloring book. These stencils had various methods of applying translucent glazes to them that would then create different effects. Sometimes a glaze in one or two colors was stippled over the outline and the design actually wiped out with

cheesecloth or something similar before the glaze dried. This would give the stencil an image similar to a Background design but more translucent. Other times, the outline would be painted in with various colors and artist's brushes, creating more of a mural effect. This type of stenciling was not for beginners and was more often found in commercial environments or homes where quality constantly emanated.

- - - - -

Does Size Really Matter?

Although size definitely can make a difference, there are other factors to consider when choosing a design for a room. After all, you want the stencil to be appropriate for the intended use. Perhaps you want to play off the architectural elements in a room, using a design of the same character such as a diamond or square pattern from leaded windows.

Here are some questions to ask yourself:

■ What type of room is it?
■ How tall are the ceilings?
■ Am I planning on doing a table linen or a wall?

Outline example, with hand-painted design.

Chances are, you can make almost any design work for your particular needs. Larger wall spaces, darker rooms and higher ceilings allow the use of stronger designs and colors. Smaller panels or walls, lighter rooms and lower ceilings generally do better with smaller or simpler designs and softer hues. The stencil should be restful to the eye and not so bold or prominent that a person feels unable to relax and rest. This is especially true in bedrooms.

So what about size anyway? A stenciled frieze should not be a prominent feature but rather something that blends into the furnishings. So how does one achieve that? You will be surprised how logical it ends up being. Let's say you have a 10-foot-tall ceiling. If you run a small design that is only a couple of inches tall along the ceiling and paint it pale pink on an off-white wall, you won't see it much at all. Unless you are having dinner parties on a ladder, most of the time folks are going to see it from a much-farther distance. Thus, taller ceilings can handle larger designs.

Now on the same order, let's say you want to stencil a table linen for Grandma. If you use that same large stencil you just used on your wall, poor Granny is going to miss out on some of the design. Therefore, a smaller design would be more appropriate. However, you may be able to use that same large design along the bottom of some portieres. Even if the large design won't work as well on Grandma's doily, that doesn't mean you can't still use it in a room, even a room with only 8-foot ceilings.

Here are a few examples of how to choose the perfect-size stencil for your project or how to make that one you-just-can't-live-without design work in your situation.

The old rule of thumb, according to various vintage stencil manuals, is that if you plan on filling a frieze area with a stencil, the design should be between 3 and 5 inches narrower than the frieze. After all, would you really use a design 3 to 5 inches wider? Keep in mind that even if you find a design that is too large, you could eliminate part of it, such as a bar or band that runs along the top

- - - - -

Chances are, you can make almost any design work for your particular needs.

- - - - -

and bottom, and it could still work. After all, adaptability is part of the beauty of stenciling. However, if the design butts up tightly against the ceiling and another element such as a picture rail, it is going to be difficult to stencil, so you'd really need that 3 to 5 inches. It gives you room in which to work easily and also allows a little freedom for when that ceiling decides to make the unexpected dip.

Since friezes can vary widely, I have broken the sizes of the stencils into four basic groups and offered some examples of other areas that are good for that particular size.

Petite and Small stencils work well for table linens.

- The Petite group consists of designs that are no larger than a couple of inches. These stencils are best used in areas where they will be viewed at a fairly short distance. Table runners and other linens may first come to mind, but these designs could easily have been used for accenting frames, women's accessories and other small decorative items. These little stencils were also used to create the outside of panels that were painted on the wall, a decorative alternative for stairways and rooms, and were a nice accent above a wainscot running around a room at mid–level, where the design would be easier to see than if placed near the ceiling.

- The Small design group is only slightly bigger than the previous group by an inch or so but these designs are a bit more substantial in their appearance. Ceiling work—accenting crown molding, following box beams or creating ceiling panels—was a common use for this group. Window curtains and larger table linens are also excellent for this size of stencil. A group of designs referred to as "Beadings" were usually in this size and were used to outline or complement wood trim in a room, forming a continuous line along baseboards or wainscoting, doors and crown molding. Beading works just as well vertically as horizontally.

- The Medium group is perhaps the most popular, with designs that are not too tiny or too big. These designs work just as well for 8-foot ceilings and larger curtains as they do for filling smaller frieze areas. Another good option is to run them above or below picture rails in bedrooms, or in any other room where that wood trim is the only treatment on the wall. This size could also be used along the edge of a bedspread or shower curtain, or part of the design could be selected and used as a Spot stencil.

- The Large group is most often seen on high ceilings and larger rooms. They can be a little more difficult to use because of their size and were most often used in commercial environments where high ceilings needed the height of a larger design. Still, if you just love one of these larger designs, there are options. Portieres are a beautiful way to bring these designs to life, or consider stenciling the design in muted tones. Above the tile wainscoting in a bathroom is also a fun and surprisingly authentic place to use some of these grand designs.

Above: *Example of beading following wainscot and continuing around a window.*

Left: *Placing the stencil at the bottom of the frieze rather than running it along the crown molding helps to lower this higher ceiling and draws attention to the lovely built-in.*

Running a stencil along the top of the wall can give the illusion of a higher ceiling. Placing the design at this height under crown molding is a nice way to accent the wood trim as well.

Above: *Taller ceilings and softer colors allow a larger design to work beautifully in this room.*

Below: *A portion of a medium design used as a Spot stencil and tucked into the painted areas of the paneling not only lightens the dark woodwork but also picks up some of the color in the pottery display.*

Stenciling wasn't always done in just a straight line. Don't forget the Spot and Panel designs, which is a Spot stencil applied to a panel or series of panels. A spot of design in the corners or open space often works where a frieze might look out of place. Rather than running a border in the dining room, consider putting a Panel design (adjusted to fit) or a medallion of design in each grass cloth or painted wainscot panel often prevalent in the bungalow interior.

Design placement and intensity of color are also factors to keep in mind. A large design or one with color that is too brilliant will emphasize the boundaries and make the room appear smaller. A smaller or simpler design and softer coloring will give the effect of greater distance. So if you want to use a larger design than you should, try stenciling it in muted colors, tone on tone perhaps. It works both ways, for if you really like that smaller design, try painting it with intense colors. Practice on paper and see what appeals to your senses.

Cut Above the Rest— Designing Your Own Stencil

Say that you can visualize the stencil of your dreams, but the problem is that you can't find it anywhere. Or perhaps you have this charming antique thingamajig and think it would be cool to have a matching stenciled doodad to go with it. There are many occasions when a custom stencil will be your preferred choice. When you learn a little about making your own stencil, you can do it right the first time before you end up recycling unwanted stencil material and chasing your spouse around the house with an Exacto knife.

Cutting the stencil is actually the easy part. It's

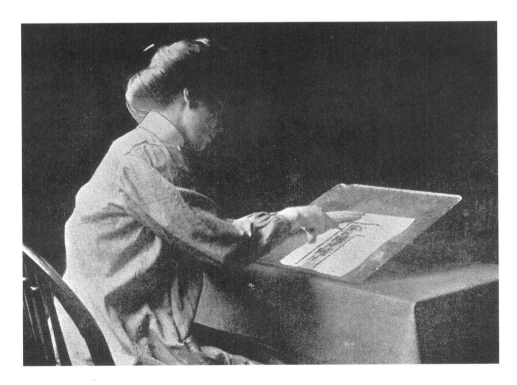

Cutting a 1908 stencil.

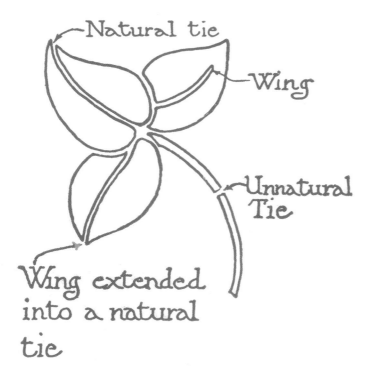

Natural tie

Wing

Unnatural Tie

Wing extended into a natural tie

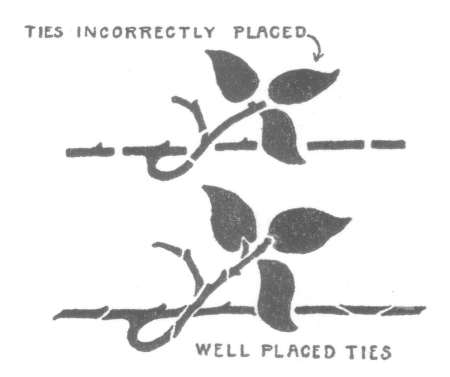

TIES INCORRECTLY PLACED

WELL PLACED TIES

the designing that can make you buggy. Consider this: you want to cut a stencil of the letter O. How would you go about doing this? It seems you'd just cut out a circle—but wait! The middle fell out!

The piece that creates the center hole in the O is referred to as a "tie" or a "bridge." These are the little strips or pieces of stencil plate that connect the larger open areas and hold the stencil plate together. Ties are an important part of the stencil. They also require some thought as to where they should be placed, as it is best to have them look as if they were meant to be part of the design. By inserting a little bridge at the top and bottom of the two circles, you will now be able to create the O.

There are good ties and bad ties. Sometimes stencils are designed with no thought or care given to placing the ties. Some stencil designers think that the stenciler would just go back over their work to fill in and obliterate where the crummy ties are. That seems like too much work to me. Besides, unless you actually cut a little "tie obliterator stencil," it is very hard to match the technique stencil brushes pro-

Vintage examples of good ties (natural), bad ties (unnatural) and wings.

When the leaf veins are turned into ties, the wings are mostly eliminated. It makes a much stronger design.

vide with a regular artist brush, especially when you are working with oils. So, instead, let's try creating good ties that you don't have to go back and eliminate.

A good tie is called a "natural" tie—these are ties that hold the stencil plate together without any apparent effort and appear naturally as part of the design. You also want to be careful of "wings" or "tabs"; those are little pieces of the stencil plate that project into a cutout area. These projections can easily be damaged but can often be extended to make contact with the other side of the opening, thus creating a more secure stencil plate by forming a tie. For instance take an oak leaf pattern, an irregular leaf with lots of lobes. This design could be full of projection problems, but by incorporating the leaf veins into ties, not only are the wings pretty much eliminated, but the design

is strengthened as well.

Designing the bridges is the trickiest part of cutting your own stencil, so here are a few tips:

- Start off by drawing your design without any bridges or ties.
- Next, go back over the design and put in the ties, concentrating on incorporating them into the pattern as much as possible. You'll do a little erasing, so keep the liquid eraser handy. If you are working with a motif from nature, look for natural areas to put a break in the design, such as the end bud of a stem where a leaf starts to protrude or other irregularities of natural growth. Plain lines can have little ornamental breaks for ties such as a dot or small square to break them up. Just like our friendly little O, a straight line can't run

- - - - -

Ties are an important part of the stencil. They also require some thought as to where they should be placed.

- - - - -

Some items needed for cutting stencils: blank material, a design, a cutting knife and mat, a ruler and a sharp marker for transferring the design.

across the bottom of a stencil without a tie or two.

- Then, use a pencil or crayon to color in all the areas that will be cut out. The object here is to expose wings or areas that still need ties.
- Now, look over the whole design again. What do you think? Are you ready to cut? Don't be discouraged if your first stencil has a tough tie or two. The only real way to become familiar with designing stencils is to cut a lot of them and learn by trial and error what makes a good design. Instead, take pencil and eraser in hand and take pride in the fact that you are

actually designing (and will soon cut) your own stencil.

Whew! The design stuff is now over and you are ready to start slicing away. Here are a few things that you will need to cut your stencil:

- Uncut blank stencil material, which is simply a piece of stencil plastic that has not been cut yet. Depending on the size of your design, you may be able to find this at your local craft store; just make sure the blank material is at least an inch larger than your design on all sides. Otherwise, go to a real artist material supply store and get a flat sheet of 5 mm acetate (or something close to it). The salesperson there should be able to direct you to a product that will work.

- A utility knife, with or without a snap-off blade. There is some advantage to the snap-off blades because you can easily break off the end of the blade, keeping it nice and sharp. Regardless of the type you use, keeping it sharp is important.
- Something to cut on. Glass works, but it dulls your knife fairly quickly. Craft and artist stores have resealing cutting mats that are very nice if you want to spend a little extra money for them. A piece of Plexiglass or even a breadboard will work if it's large enough. Before you buy, see what you have around that might work.

When you are finished tracing, you will once again want to fill in or somehow indicate the areas to be cut out. If you don't want to take the time to fill in the whole area, at least draw lines or mark the spaces with a big X to easily show the cutting areas. Remove the design from the back of the plastic. Now you are ready to start the cutting process.

Some folks like to skip the process of retracing the design onto the plastic by simply leaving the design taped to the back of the blank material and allowing that to be the guide rather than the marker outline. This is fine, but keep in mind that you will most likely destroy the paper design and the paper underneath as you cut through the plastic. If you plan on using this method, be wise and make at least one copy of your original design, just in case.

To begin, hold the cutting knife at a 45 degree angle from the blank material. I like to press my

---

Don't be discouraged if your first stencil has a tough tie or two.

- A fine-tip marker, to transfer the design to the stencil plastic.
- Tape, to hold your design to the plastic.
- A ruler.

Take the stencil material and lay it on top of your new design. Make sure the design is at least an inch from the edge of the material on all sides. Use one of the straight edges of the material as a guide; running your design parallel to it is much handier than having to level the design after the fact. Tape the design to the back of the plastic so it won't shift while you transfer the image to the front with the marker. Now flip the material over and trace the design onto the plastic with the marker.

middle finger against the edge of the blade to apply pressure when cutting, but you may find another position more comfortable. One of the best tips I can give you is to keep your cutting utensil very sharp. If you are using an Exacto knife, you will want to change the blade when it seems like it is not cutting as well; be aware that this could be several times, depending on the size of the stencil. Those slender little plastic utility knives are not only inexpensive but are very easy to keep constantly sharp by snapping off the blade at the first sign that it is getting dull. Razor blades are better left for shaving purposes. As for electric stencil cutters, they often end up being more work than necessary since they leave a melted beaded

Trace the design onto the plastic with a fine-tipped marker.

edge that needs to be removed to create a sharp edge before stenciling can commence.

Start by cutting out the smaller areas, especially on larger stencils. It is harder to cut these areas when the larger adjacent areas have been cut previously, thereby weakening the stencil.

Pulling the knife toward you will make the cutting easier. Try turning the stencil material for curved areas rather than attempting to bend your hand in unnatural ways. And stop short before cutting the end of a curve; instead, rotate the design

and come at it from the opposite angle. This can save a bridge or tie from an unmerciful sacrifice.

Also keep in mind that if you cut the lines with a straightedge but cut the rest by hand, it will look out of place. Instead, do your best at cutting straight lines by hand. This will lend uniformity to the stencil and give it more character as well. After all, you are creating a stencil by hand. These slight imperfections only contribute to the testimony of doing so.

Hold the cutting knife at a 45 degree angle from the blank material. Stop short before cutting the end of a curve. Instead rotate the design and come at it from the opposite angle.

Conjuring Up a Paint Medium

There are three things you need to have in order to stencil. Obviously, the first is a stencil. It doesn't really matter whether you have purchased a precut stencil or designed and cut your own; if you are stenciling a floral motif or simply signage on a shipping crate, you can't stencil without a stencil. The second item needed is some kind of paint medium. Finally, you need something to transfer the paint to the stencil plate through the openings and onto the surface you are stenciling.

Basically there are two choices when it comes to selecting a paint medium to work with: oil-based and water-based paint. In my years of experience in stenciling and using stencil products, I have only three words to say regarding water-based

Congratulations! You've cut a stencil.

paints for stenciling, especially if you have never stenciled before—don't use them. Despite the popularity of water-based paints in the majority of stencil books written in the 1970s when ducks with bows were all the rage, oil-based paints go along with many of the vintage books written about Arts and Crafts–period stenciling. I found through my hands-on workshops that beginners achieve quicker and better results with the oil-based mediums than with the water-based paints, which they often find more challenging to work with.

Time and time again, I've listened to some unhappy stenciler mutter discouraging tales of a previous project, vowing never to stencil again. The first thing I always ask them is what kind of paint they used. More often than not, the offensive medium was water-based. I cannot fault those who have chosen this type of paint to work with in their first project. After all, in our modern world we rarely use oil-based paints for interior projects, so it does seem logical that a water-based paint would be the easiest to use. It dries fast, you can wash out your brushes with water, the smell is less repulsive, and so forth. To be honest, there may be certain situations where one might find a water-based paint preferable to oil, but I find these are usually the exceptions. With that said, let's examine in more detail the advantages of oil over water when it comes to choosing a paint medium. If you still insist on using water-based paint, we'll look at how to make it go a little smoother.

Oil: Not the Slick Devil You Imagined

Because oil-based mediums don't set up or dry as fast, it is easier to manipulate these paints. For this reason the blending and shading techniques often found in this style of vintage stenciling are much easier to create. The paint can actually be layered to create more depth or shading within one color or to blend a seam where two colors come together, creating a beautiful transition between the two. Softer, more translucent images can be achieved by applying less paint with a little more pressure. Of course, if you desire a solid opaque pattern, simply apply the paint a little heavier. Although one of the advantages to the oil paint is its extended setup time, this dry-brush technique as it is called, uses so little paint that it allows you to readily move the stencil plate without the worry of depositing wet paint where it is unwanted. Unless you have applied an extremely heavy coat of oil paint, it will usually be absolutely dry within 24 hours.

There are several forms of oil-based paint mediums available on the market. No longer do you need to mix your dry pigments with linseed oil in an old milk can, manufacturing your own paint

Beginners achieve quicker and better results with the oil-based mediums than with water-based paints . . .

on-site just so you can stencil. Two forms of "solid" oils available on the market today are paint sticks that resemble a jumbo crayon or little plastic pots filled with what is referred to as "crème" paint. I prefer the sticks because I find it is easier to control the amount of paint you put on your brush when you are lifting it from a scribble on a palette.

The crème paints require you to dip your brush directly into the little pot of paint where you are more likely to overload it. However, the sticks can sometimes be more difficult to find and may not come in all the colors you imagined in your dream stencil, so in these cases, the little pots suffice. Another form of paint stick that is often available

After choosing a stencil, you need to decide on what other materials you will want to use.

With a sharp knife or razor blade or by rubbing with a paper towel, peel off the protective skin that forms.

Rub the stick onto a palette that has a smooth nonporous surface.

through artist supply stores is called an oil bar, but I find these to be much greasier and can cause an oily "shadow" on certain projects. Unless you are extra careful or more experienced with this medium, I recommend you avoid it. Artist oils in tubes can be a challenge, again because they can be greasy, but if you are feeling adventurous, give it a shot. No matter which type of paint medium you use, do some practicing before applying it to your final project.

Regardless of the form of "solid" oil paint you work with, first you will need to peel off the protective skin that forms (kind of like on pudding) with a sharp knife or razor blade, or by rubbing with a paper towel. I like using a utility knife, extending the snap-off blade about an inch and peeling the paint stick like a carrot. Only remove the skin about half an inch down the stick; you can always remove more if necessary. Since so little paint is used with the solid oils, this should usually suffice for one day of work. The skin will reform after about 24 hours, sealing the paint again and keeping it fresh for future use. Some of the paint sticks come with a handy cardboard sleeve that helps keep your fingers clean and can easily be loosened at the seam when it needs to be pushed back as the paint stick wears down. If you are using the little plastic pots of paint, you will still need to remove the skin from the top of the paint. This can be a little trickier than peeling a paint stick, but it still needs to be done. Try using a butter knife (so you won't cut yourself as you jab away) and attempt to lift it from the

Sparingly apply the paint to the stencil brush by picking up some of the paint from one of the edges of the scribbled area on the palette, keeping the brush at a 90 degree angle. Work it into the bristles in a circular motion on a dry area of the palette to evenly distribute the paint over the end of the bristles.

Using very little pressure, apply the paint to an opening on the stencil plate, starting around the edges and working in towards the center.

edge. Some like using a paper towel. Experiment and discover what works best for you.

After the skin has been removed, rub the stick onto a palette that has a smooth nonporous surface. Wax-coated paper or plastic plates and smooth-surface microwave dishes are some examples of typical household items that can be used as palettes (but you may not want to eat off them again). Many folks are familiar with the old plastic

a very light coat of paint to start with. Too much paint applied too quickly and with too much pressure results in paint buildup along the edges that will cause bleeding and smudging as you move the stencil plate. What you want is a nice balance between how much paint is on your brush and how much pressure you are using to apply the paint. The best results are achieved with less paint and more pressure. If you want the image

- - - - -

What you want is a nice balance between how much paint is on your brush and how much pressure you are using to apply the paint.

- - - - -

Melamine dishware. This stuff works well for a palette because the smooth nonporous surface is easy to clean off, rigid and doesn't flex in your hand during use. You do not want to apply the paint stick directly to the wall, like a crayon. The excessive paint will create a buildup that causes smudging of the stencil print as you move it along, and you will just end up with a mess on your hands, on the stencil plate and on the wall.

When you are ready to transfer the paint to the stencil openings, apply the paint sparingly to the stencil brush by picking up some of the paint from the edge of the scribbled area on the palette. Work it into the bristles in a circular motion on a dry area of the palette, keeping the brush at a 90 degree angle. This will evenly distribute the paint over the ends of the bristles. Using very little pressure, apply the paint to an opening on the stencil plate, starting around the edges and working in towards the center. Experiment using a stippling (a tapping or pouncing motion) or a swirling motion. Apply

darker, apply a second coat with a little more pressure, using more paint if necessary. Practicing on paper will help you learn how to apply the paint by using a method you feel comfortable with and will also help you learn how to avoid overworking the same area again and again.

- - - - -

If You Must Use Acrylics . . .

As I said before, I understand why a person would consider using a water-based paint to stencil with, but the whole "ease of use" is actually a misconception. I'm sure there are situations when it is the medium of choice, although I have a tough time coming up with many where oil-based paint wouldn't be just as good or better. Perhaps I shouldn't be so hard on this type of paint. To be honest, once you learn some of the tricks of the

- - - - -

No matter which type of paint medium you use, do some practicing before applying it to your final project.

- - - - -

trade, acrylics can be much easier to deal with. I still firmly believe that they are harder for the beginner to handle, but think of it this way—a beginner doesn't know any better. If you insist on using water-based paints, at least let me shed a little light on the situation and offer a few tips.

Most of the time, the water-based paint is really runny—latex paint from a can or a little bottle of something from the craft store. If this is the form of paint you intend to use, be prepared to waste a lot of it. Because so little paint is used to stencil with, when you use a runny, water-based acrylic medium, you need to remove about 90 percent of it from your brush before it ever gets to the stencil plate. An over-loaded brush oozes paint under the stencil plate and creates a blurry, messy effect. This is where most people succumb and give up on stenciling. So how can you conquer the acrylic? After barely dipping your brush into the smallest amount of paint, you will still have way too much paint on your brush. Dab the brush on several pieces of paper toweling to remove most of the paint, creating a "dry" brush. Test the brush on the stencil plate first by dabbing the brush on the outer plastic (not near an opening). You'll want to see a thin film of paint. If the brush leaves a glob that looks like it could run, go back to the paper towels and remove more paint. Learning how little paint you need on your brush to start with is like learning a secret password.

With water-based paint, you will probably find a stippling motion works best to transfer the paint to the stencil openings. Apply the paint, going beyond the cutout area and onto the stencil plate a little way. Pulling the paint from the stencil plate into an opening will help to prevent the buildup along the edge that causes the image to lose its crispness.

Besides running, water-based paints or acrylics dry too fast. As they start to dry, they tend to bond with the stencil plate, which means you need to wash it frequently. The more you have to clean off your stencil, the more likely you are to damage it. To me, this is about as convenient as matching and folding socks from the dryer. Also, as the paint starts to dry on the brush, it has a tendency to get sticky or gummy. Washing the brush often (more socks from the dryer) may help with the gumming up. Be sure to thoroughly dry a wet brush before reusing it because the excess water can further dilute the already-runny paint. Well, you see how this can get frustrating in a hurry.

One of the simplest tricks you can do is to keep a spray bottle and extra paper towels within easy reach as you stencil. By frequently misting the brush and rubbing any excess onto a paper towel, it prolongs the time it takes the brush to gum up. By keeping the brush flexible, it is easier to pull the excess paint into the openings, thus keeping your stencil plate cleaner as well. This is a bit easier said than done, but it is by no means brain surgery. A rag moistened with isopropyl alcohol can also be used to keep brushes from gumming up, but make sure the paint you are using is compatible with it. Remember, you want to keep your brush moist, not wet. A little practice and you will soon see how well you can control the infamous acrylic headaches.

If you are going to use water-based paints, pre- pare for the problems that arise because of their quick drying times. Be careful of going over an area too many times, for as the acrylic paint starts to set, it can bond with the fresh paint and pop off the wall, creating areas that are difficult to touch up. They definitely do not give you as much free- dom to blend and shade as the oil-based paints do, but there is indeed hope. With all these shortcuts and tips and a little practice, you are well on your way to conquering the art of stenciling.

Barely dip your brush into a small amount of paint and blot the brush on several pieces of paper, toweling to remove most of the paint, thereby creating a "dry" brush.

Apply the paint, going beyond the cutout area and onto the stencil plate a little way. To help prevent buildup along the edge, which causes the image to lose crispness, pull the paint from the stencil plate into an opening.

Apply Yourself (or the Stencil Paint)

Got the stencil? Check. Found the paint? Check. Now let's get the two together. Even if you just wanted to throw paint-filled balloons at a stencil tacked up on the inside of the garage, you still need a vehicle to transport the paint to the stencil opening. Rather than a balloon, I suggest a stencil brush, although a balloon toss might release the creative inner child in all of us.

Stencil brushes are definitely the most widely used applicator in this decorative form of art. The best brushes of all times are constructed from natural hog bristles. Notice that the ends of the stencil brushes are flat; if stood on the ends of their bristles, they would not fall over. Good brushes have the soft rounded natural edges of the hair perfectly aligned, whereas cheaper brushes have cut off the hairs to form the flat edge. The sole purpose in the life of this particular type of brush is to stencil, so you want to make sure you use them properly. The brushes should be held at a 90 degree angle, perpendicular to the surface they are retrieving paint from or depositing it on. The flat end prevents the bristles from sliding under the stencil plate, thus giving the design a sharp crisp edge.

I suppose once upon a time that stencil brush bristles were originally made short so as to keep from splaying out as they were tapped and pushed around. Even today I wonder why they are not made with shorter bristles. Alas, they are not and so as one stencils away, the hairs spread out where they may as pressure on them is increased. However, there is a perfectly good solution to this little inconvenience—tape. Use a piece of masking tape long enough to make several wraps around the bristles, allowing about a quarter of an inch of the end of the brush bristles to show. I prefer to use the lower-tack painter's tape, as it is easier on the bristles when it is removed, but regular masking tape is acceptable. Remember to remove the tape before you clean the brush. Also a rubber band could be wrapped around the ends of the bristles, again leaving a quarter of an inch or so of the bristles showing to provide flexibility.

I originally thought using tape was a modern-day adaptation to the stencil brush until I read about it in some of my vintage stencil catalogs. This simple solution not only gives one much more control over the stencil brush, it also has a tendency to keep the brush cleaner as the paint has a more difficult time working its way down into the ferrule of the brush.

Plan on having a separate brush for each color you are working with in your stencil. As long as you

Get a piece of masking tape long enough to wrap around the brush several times and allow about 1/4-inch of the bristles to show. This gives more control over the stencil brush and keeps the bristles cleaner.

take care of your brushes, you can reuse them on many stenciling projects for many years to come. I found that brushes are really a personal choice, and so to determine the correct size, just experiment to see what suits you best. I know that statement does seem like a cop-out, so I'll explain.

The larger the brush, the faster you will go. However, you still may need to maintain color separation when necessary. For this reason, I recommend having a variety of sizes to start with. Sometimes actually having two brushes in one color will make the job go faster, a larger one to apply the color quickly and a smaller one to get in the tighter areas. A larger brush makes color separation more difficult because it can cause too much unwanted overflow into other areas. Don't use a too small brush in a large area either. It simply takes too long. Remember back to that garage-sale sign you once made when you used a large stinky marker to fill in the oversized letters so the cars would see it? Remember the little marker marks left behind? The result is the same when you use a tiny brush and a large stencil opening.

There are a few other types of applicators, although they are not as popular and deliver different effects. If you are doing a stencil in one color in a water-based paint medium, high up where you may not see all the little imperfections, using a sponge or foam roller are options. Keep in mind that you need to once again be careful of using too much runny paint that could seep under the stencil plate. Using rollers will definitely go faster than using several different colored stencil brushes but it will also have none of the character. However, it is a valid option and if you are unhappy with the result, you can always paint over it. Airbrushing has also gained in popularity, but unless you have an airbrush, it may take you longer to become familiar with that tool than if you were to just use stencil brushes. Of course, if you have done some airbrushing, you could give this a try. Finally, I hesitate to even bring up that brief stint in stenciling when aerosol cans of paint were used. Just the smell and the idea of masking off areas convinced me to forgo that technique. The thing to remember is this—if something intrigues you, try it. After all, it's just a coat of paint, and if the results don't please you, then follow with another coat.

- - - - -

Assorted Fun in the Sundries

All the pieces are in place now—the stencil, some paint medium and something with which to apply the paint. These may be the mandatory items, but there are assorted sundries that should be mentioned.

Sometimes actually having two brushes in one color makes the job go faster. A larger green brush will cover the leaves and stems more quickly but may be too large to do the base of the flower. Having a smaller green brush to get into the tighter areas allows for color separation without slowing things down.

These are little things you might not think about, but they are definitely worthwhile to consider before beginning your stenciling project.

First, you need something to attach the stencil to whatever you are planning on stenciling—be it a wall or a piece of fabric. Some of the old manuals suggest simply holding the stencil in place, but unless you are stenciling one tiny doily for Grandma, you are asking for problems.

In my vintage stenciling catalogs and manuals, I found it odd that even though they mentioned the taping of brushes, they don't suggest using tape to hold the stencil in place. Small pins seemed to be the adhesion of choice back then. Today, some diehards or those who are unfamiliar with stenciling still insist on using tape to secure the stencil in place. Fortunately, we are the beneficiaries of a wonderful modern-day product referred to as stencil adhesive. This aerosol glue is sprayed over the back of a stencil, turning it into a great big Post-It note that you can pull on and off with ease. One thing to note: there are many forms of adhesive in an aerosol can, so make sure the label says it is repositionable and be sure to shake the can well before you use it. This adhesive allows you to realign the stencil plate over and over without recoating. Simply put a light coat on the back of the stencil and allow it to dry. This only takes a few minutes. Lightly recoat it whenever the stencil starts to loose tack. There is no need for excessive spraying—this isn't a 1950s hairdo. As long as you let the repositionable adhesive set up for about two minutes after you spray it, you don't have to worry about leaving a residue behind on the stenciled surface.

I cannot stress enough the need to practice with your materials before you head to your final project. And there have been so many times that I've talked with first-time stencilers who grabbed their stencil, paint and brushes and headed for the most dominant spot on the living room wall to attempt their first stencil pattern. I know you can just paint over it, but please use a little bit of common sense and have some fun experimenting on paper first. Get a roll of freezer-wrap paper from the grocery store (in the baggie section) and go

the wall is darker, say a sage green, paint a piece of poster board with two coats of the same wall paint and then do your sample on that. Trim it and tape that to the wall. This is a great way to get good quick visuals without actually putting any paint on the surface. Believe me, a stencil looks quite a bit different at ten feet than at the two feet, especially if it is on a darker color.

You can feel confident about following any wood trim or tile with your stencil. Even if it is not level, it is still best to follow it or you will just accentuate the amount it varies. But following an untrimmed ceiling is a different story. The easiest way to mark an area to stencil is to snap a chalk line or use a level. Laser levels are all the rage now,

- - - - -

I cannot stress enough the need to practice with your materials before you head to your final project.

- - - - -

wild. Try different colors in different areas of the stencil; experiment with the brush sizes and which size you like working with best in the various areas. Who cares what the paper samples look like or how many you do. Try different things.

When you finally come up with the perfect example, do a three-foot section so you have at least a couple of repeats. Then take that chunk of sample paper and tape it up on the wall or pin it to your curtains—wherever you are planning on using it. Let it sit there for a day or so and every time you walk into the room and see it, pay attention to your gut reaction. It will tell you a lot. Should it be higher, lower or is it just right? How about the color? Need a little more green? If so, do another sample and tape it up. If the color of

are easy to use and have really come down in cost; if you can get your hands on one of these cool tools, do so. However, the old-fashioned method of snapping a chalk line still works well. If you are unfamiliar with chalk lines, they are much easier to do with another person, so choose a helper who is familiar with this technique. You can use a regular level as well, but make sure it is at least three feet; the little torpedo levels are fine for hanging pictures, but don't count on them for a ten-foot stretch of wall.

Even with oil-based paints, the only time you really need to use paint thinner or mineral spirits for cleaning is when you are ready to remove the stencil adhesive from the back of the stencil. It is not necessary to remove the adhesive off the back if your project takes several days. Simply lay the sticky side of the stencil on the shiny side of butcher paper or wax paper and store it on the bag it came in temporarily. However, you should remove the adhesive before storing your stencil for the long term. You will also want to remove the adhesive if you are planning on using your stencil in a mirror image application. You can easily remove it with paper toweling moistened with paint thinner. Again, be careful of the delicate stencil bridges and tabs as you wipe it. Don't scrimp on the paper towels when doing this; when one gums up, get a new one. It will make the job faster and easier.

Whether you are using oil- or water-based paints though, I highly recommend a brush cleaner called The Masters Brush Cleaner and Preserver for cleaning and reconditioning your brushes. It is a nontoxic product similar in use to shaving soap and works with any paint medium. I have even used this on my poor little abused demo brushes after a show. It is surprising how it brings them back to life. This just goes to show that taking care of the brushes will make them last forever, and sometimes even when they are neglected a little. This cleaner is also great for removing paint-stick spots that happen to make their way on to places where they aren't intended to go.

In short, buy quality items and take care of them. You will find it makes your tasks much easier and they pay for themselves in the long run. This was something I finally learned when I was building my house. Coming from a superbly disorganized pack-rat family, I often saw my father buy another cheap widget because he couldn't find the other five he owned. When my husband and I built our house, he insisted on purchasing a fabulously expensive table saw, one that took a lot of persuasion to buy and made my carpenter father drool. We could have purchased a cheaper one, but we chose to invest in the better tool. I saw our project accomplished much easier due to purchasing a quality tool, and by taking care of it, the old table saw continues to produce many a fine item to this day.

Of course a table saw contains a few more zeros in its price than a stencil brush, but the lesson is basically the same. The extra amount for quality items is worth every penny.

- - - - -

Color Your World

I wonder how many people really have any idea about how much color affects their lives. Curious as to why the big boss always wears a black suit? Do you realize a certain hamburger joint picked a certain color for their servers' uniforms because it tends to make you hungry? Color definitely affects our moods. It can motivate you, perk you up or calm you down. There are warm colors and cool colors that can greatly benefit a room, depending on what side of the house the room is on and the amount of light it receives. Plus there are some handy little tips that can be used to help you choose colors that go well together.

Let's start with Color 101. Learning a bit about color can be helpful in easing the anxiety of which colors should be used where. First, we have the primary colors of red, yellow and blue. Think of these as the first generation of colors, the Adam and Eve of pigment. There is also white, the absence of color, and black, the total of all colors. If you have been to a paint store and tried to decide on one color out of the gazillion cards with paint color samples on them, you'll immediately understand how many colors can be mixed from a combination of the three primary colors and a little white or black. Amazing, isn't it? Once that concept is clear, it's time to introduce you to the legendary color wheel.

The traditional color wheel is a circle divided into six sections, like a pie. In every other section, one of the three primary colors resides. The empty section between the primary colors is for what are called secondary colors. They are made by combining the two primaries on either side. For example, if the primary color red is combined with the primary color yellow, the secondary color will be orange. Red with blue produces the secondary violet, more commonly known as purple. Finally, the other two primaries, blue and yellow, make the secondary green. All the colors in the color wheel are red, orange, yellow, green, blue and violet. Simple, isn't it? So where do the fun and funky colors like teal, cranberry, peach, and periwinkle come into the color wheel?

It's possible to expand the color wheel to include a wider range of colors. Imagine another wheel similar to the one described previously. However, this new wheel has twelve pie shapes this time, with the same primary and secondary colors. But now there is an empty slot left in between each of the colors. So what to do with those empty places? Make new colors, of course! By mixing a primary color with a secondary color, the tertiary or intermediate colors are created—red-orange,

The Arts and Crafts movement used colors found in nature, bringing those tranquil hues into the home. Take a walk and see what colors inspire you.

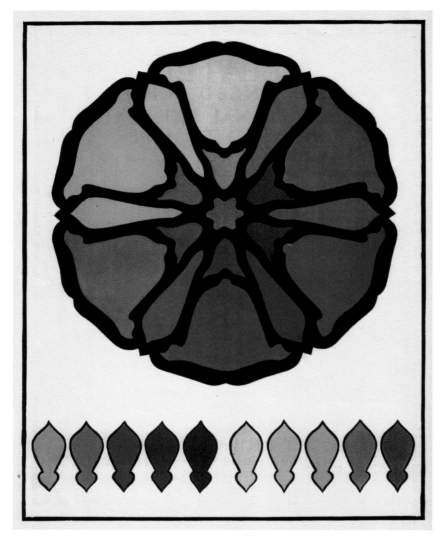

Adding white creates tints, and adding black creates shades. This color wheel uses blue and orange to demonstrate.

Believe it or not, there IS a difference. The first color in the name indicates the dominant color, and if you were mixing these colors on a palette, you would definitely see a difference between an orange you have added red to and a red you have added orange to.

So you might be thinking to yourself that this color mixing is no big deal and that you mastered that art back in kindergarten. But wait! There is more.

A color has three main characteristics. *Hue* is basically another name for the color family it belongs to; a color's *intensity* (or if you want to get real fancy, *chroma*) indicates how bright or dull a color is; and *value* determines how light or dark a color is. By altering the intensity and value of a color or hue, we can create a multitude of colors, hence the hundreds and hundreds of paint store sample cards.

By adding white and black, a color's value can vary. For instance, take the color blue. I can create a midnight blue or a soft pale baby blanket blue by simply adding white or black and still stay within the same position on the color wheel. Add white to one of the hues on your color wheel and you will have what is called a *tint*. White reduces the strength of a color and makes it appear more opaque. Add black to one of your colors and you will create a *shade*, reducing the color's vividness and darkening it. Many of the colors available on the market today have white or black as part of their makeup. But in

yellow-orange, yellow-green—you get the idea. If you really want to go crazy with the color wheel, you can add more sets of blank pie pieces and continue mixing adjacent colors and creating new hues until a full spectrum of color is produced. Pretty soon, you will have red, red-orange, orange-red, orange, orange-yellow, yellow-orange, and so forth. At that level, you may start to wonder what the difference really is between red-orange and orange-red.

mixing a tint or shade, it is easy to just end up with a muddy or dirty color. If you want to tone down a color, there is a better option.

Let's go back to the color wheel. The colors directly opposite each other on the color wheel are referred to as complementary colors. These colors react strongly with each other, and as they play off each other, they appear more vibrant. They are aesthetically pleasing to gaze upon as well. Because they are so strongly opposed (think of them as Democrats and Republicans), they can work extremely well together (unlike Democrats and Republicans) when it comes to mixing colors. If a color appears too intense, some people immediately add black to tone it down. However, black is a strong color and, more often than not, ends up making the color appear dirty. Mixing in the complementary color will make the original color appear less vibrant while still keeping the hue fresh and clean.

The color wheel can also be a helpful tool and can keep you entertained for lengthy periods of time as you learn about the various ways the colors can combine in aesthetically pleasing ways. But before you get to that point you will want to decide what your main color will be or, in other words, what color you want to dominate the room. Rather than just pull a white rabbit (or tint thereof) out of your hat, here are a few more things to consider about color.

The legendary color wheel, where all colors emerge from the three primary colors of red, blue and yellow.

- - - - -

Feeling Blue or in the Pink: How Colors Affect Us

Suppose we talk about how colors make you feel. Go ahead and stretch out on the couch as you ponder that. I understand you may have an aversion to some color that goes back to your childhood, but you'll have to figure that one out on your own. When you walk into a room, one of the first things you notice is the room's color, whether you consciously notice it or not. From a tranquil walk in the woods to that blue bedroom you could never get rid of as a child, color will trigger memories and feelings. Since colors affect our moods, let's look at how you can make color work to your advantage.

First, there are warm colors (reds, oranges and yellows) and cool colors (greens, blues and violets). The names are logical—red-hot coals, iceberg blue. As always, there are some exceptions to the rule. Keep in mind that on the color wheel, colors are in a circle so a cool hue can be made warmer as it moves towards the warmer spectrum and vice versa.

Warm colors have a tendency to energize and stimulate, especially red. Yellow elevates the mood and is a good color for anywhere you need a little "sunshine." Orange stimulates the appetite so you might want to reevaluate using it in the TV room if you're trying to shed a few pounds. It may be perfect in the northeast room that always has a chill in winter. The cool colors are naturally soothing. Think of the blues and greens seen in nature. Green has a tendency to be calming; violet evokes peaceful feelings and has the potential to induce sleep. In a warm climate, blues can evoke a more comfortable living environment. With the neutrals, white can evoke a sense of purity and cleanliness but can also feel very sterile. Black, often a color associated with negative images like "the black plague of death," also reflects a much more positive side with elegance, wealth and a sense of power, as in "black tie." Of course, color affects everyone differently and just because green provides a tranquil space for one, it may remind another of an undesirable "green streak."

The most important thing that matters when you are dealing with the effects of color is how a particular color affects you personally. How does it make you feel? No two people see the same color in exactly the same way. You need to trust your instincts and realize that you are much more capable of choosing colors that make you feel good. After all, who knows better what you like than you?

When it comes to choosing your colors, ask yourself a few questions. What size is the room? What time of the day does this room get the most use and who will be using it? Which direction does the room face and will the amount of natural light it receives make a difference? And just because there are certain guidelines here you can

- - - - -

Since colors affect our moods, let's look at how you can make color work to your advantage.

- - - - -

This yellow kitchen nook is warm and inviting, especially on a snowy winter day. How does the same nook in blue make you feel?

follow, if you really want a periwinkle bathroom, you can have one. But you may determine how much the periwinkle dominates the room by the answers to these questions.

Color can also affect the appearance of a room in others ways. Warm colors can appear to reduce the size of the room when used with strong values, causing the painted area to advance. Cool colors recede and make the room look larger. Keep this in mind when you are deciding on what color to paint the ceiling. For example an 11-foot ceiling can handle a darker color that gives it the illusion of being not quite as high, but you probably won't want to use that same dark color on a low ceiling in a finished basement. I have a funny little bathroom in my office that has wainscot paneling to about 4 1/2 feet with 11-foot ceilings. It is like a shoebox on its end. To bring the ceiling down, the walls above the wainscot and the ceiling are painted the same color, which is darker than the white wainscot. To bring

The thing to remember is this—
if something intrigues you, try it.

it even lower, a tall stencil design is painted right above the wainscot. All of this fools the eye, keeping it from being drawn endlessly upward. Had I run a border around the top of the wall, it would have only emphasized the disproportional height and, more likely than not, gotten lost in the process.

Start Scheming (with Color)

Choosing your color scheme may be one of the most daunting parts of decorating your home, but I have some tips to make it easier. Always pleasing and easy to achieve, the monochromatic combination is simply using different values of the same color; pick a hue and a tint and shade of that same color. Equally safe is working with a range of neutral colors, you know—whites, beiges, browns or grays with perhaps a touch of black. You can accent with a favorite color as well. Personally, I like color and find working with various simple pale

This illustration of the Martynia, popularly called "unicorn plant," provides some variations of related color-wheel combinations.

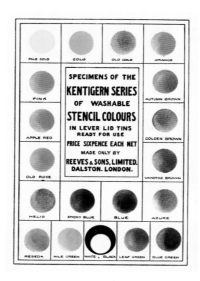
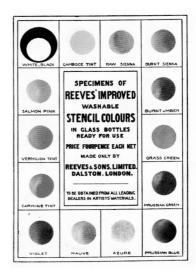

shades of white perfectly boring. Besides, it does absolutely nothing to bring out the beauty of natural wood-work. Keep that in mind if you have a splendid little bungalow with lots of glorious unpainted natural wood trim and built-ins. If you want to stay neutral, at least consider picking out a brown or gold that has some value

But for color, let's return to the color wheel one more time for some ideas. Similar colors appear close to each other on the color wheel, like green and blue, and are a pretty safe bet. Don't forget the complementary colors (opposites on the wheel, like red and green). A variation is called a split complementary and uses a color along with the hues flanking the complementary, say blue-violet with yellow and orange. It may at first sound odd, but you would be surprised at the outcome. Then there's the "triad," three colors equally spaced from each other—like the primary colors of red, yellow and blue. With the various formulas connected to the color wheel,

A London stencil catalog manufacturer shows a color chart with a limited number of washable oil colors available in tins or glass bottles.

Many glaze and stencil colors were available from Sherwin-Williams at about the same time. Still many colors continued to be custom-mixed on-site.

it can be a helpful tool in finding other options to use with that color you just can't live without.

I remember doing a job for a client who was an elementary school art teacher. We had decided on one color for the stencil project and using my trusty color wheel, I showed him the other two colors I planned on using. He looked at me as if I had bugs crawling out of my head, so I asked him to just trust me on this. Surprisingly, he did. When I provided the sample board to him, he loved it and the room came out spectacularly. I cannot stress enough the importance of doing paper samples and experimenting, especially when you are working with a color wheel. Sometimes colors that you would not believe could possibly work together can produce wonderful results. You just might be pleasantly surprised. Even if you aren't pleased and end up throwing your samples in the trash, who cares? It's only a piece of paper. Play with colors until you get the combination you love.

Unless you are going with a monochromatic scheme, your colors will look best if they are in the same value range. Seeing colors in the form of their value (how light or dark the color is) may take a little getting used to. Try picturing the room as a black-and-white photo, or better yet, take a photo for reference. Another idea that may prove helpful is to stick within the same "row" on the paint sample cards you pick up from your hardware store or paint dealer.

Here's an old interior designer trick. Consider working off the colors from something that will be in the room, say the drapery or upholstery fabrics, or a collection of pottery. It is much easier to match the paint for your wall to an item than to find the perfect item to match your unusual shade of magenta. Painting the walls the same as the background of some fabric and incorporating the other fabric colors into a stencil and other decorative items in the room works wonderfully. It's a simple way to pick out a color scheme.

By now, you likely have all kinds of ideas spinning around in your head and you are even more confused about picking out colors than when we started. Take a hike, literally. The whole idea surrounding the decorative arts of the Arts and Crafts movement was to incorporate the soothing effects of nature into the home. Go visit Mother Nature and observe her in a whole new way. Check out the trees, the rocks, and the water. What colors dominate the landscape? When you start paying attention to the colors that surround you, you'll be surprised how talented that old girl is.

- - - - -

Be an Original

We are so spoiled in this day and age. It makes me wonder what a painter during the turn of the nineteenth century would think about the color palette available to us today. Some of the paint cards or charts from my vintage stencil catalogs only offer a dozen or so colors to choose from. Quite often paints were mixed on-site using pigments and some kind of binder to make them fluid and make the paint viable. Recipes for mixing paint colors were offered to help the contractor come up with what was desired. One book has twenty-seven formulas just to create various blues. For instance, to produce a misty blue at that time, it took fifty parts of white lead paint, ten parts of ultramarine blue and one part of burnt umber. Cool, but who says that what I think of as a misty blue is the same color that the author was feeling at the time. Or that one painter added just a little more burnt umber than another. Thus, on-site mixing caused the colors to vary enormously. Today, Alizarin Crimson is going to look pretty similar, no matter who is producing it, but if you felt like mixing it with a few parts of white lead, that could change things a bit.

Without mixing a color to match on-site, it can be hard to tell someone the exact colors that they should use to recapture that vintage stencil they just discovered underneath five layers of wallpaper.

But that certainly doesn't mean they can't recapture the beauty of the stencil. Most of the time, the original stencils I run across are damaged beyond restoration. Over the years, things like paint and wallpaper paste, cracks from settling, and water damage push original stencils to a realm beyond salvation. Rather than take on the difficult job of restoring the stencil, often the best solution is to document it, reclaim the wall and put the stencil back in. If the original design and the colors still work in the room, you should be able to get pretty close to the original color without having to go to the trouble of custom mixing.

Remember, just because the original stencil was a certain color, you are now the present occupant. Unless there is some incredible significance to the stencil, like the stencil and specific colors were specced in by some famous architect when designing the house, you shouldn't lose any sleep over adding a little yellow to that original brown-pink that you don't really care for. Many, many stencils were originally ordered by mail and painted by the homeowner; therefore, if you don't care for it, it is your right to alter or change it. Just don't start painting the original unpainted woodwork. For any Arts and Crafts homeowner, that's taboo and a flogging may be in order. ■

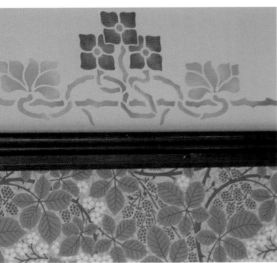

The colors in these two stencil designs were custom-mixed to match Bradbury & Bradbury wallpapers the owners had chosen.

Preparation and Application

ike most people, layout and preparation seem unnecessary in order to get to stenciling. But the time and effort put into preparation pays off in the end because the work goes easier and the outcome looks better. The time taken in the layout eliminates the minor and not so minor glitches one can run into. So clench your fists, grit your teeth and whine a little if you want, but just deal with it. Of course, you can wing it, but at least review these helpful tips to see how a little extra effort can make that undesirable preparation time go more smoothly.

Laying Out Your Design

For most types of stencils, a basic layout using some kind of horizontal guide is necessary. This may be a chair rail, wainscoting, a picture rail,

crown molding or the edge of the tile in a bathroom. Be cautious of using the ceiling as a guide though and NEVER trust that a ceiling is level. You can place a straight level in various spots along your ceiling using the bubble on the level to determine if your ceiling is even. If most of the ceiling seems to be level, you can follow it, but you will have to account for the occasional dip by keeping your pattern straight rather than by following the irregularities in the ceiling. If the ceiling is quite uneven you will need to create a level horizontal guideline to follow.

The simplest way to get a horizontal guide is by having something like a picture rail or wainscoting that someone has already leveled and provided for you. Alas, if you have a plain wall without any guideline, it will be up to you to create one, using a variety of methods. Let's start with the level.

A level is like a board with a glass bubble tube inside. When the bubble is matched up to a line marked on the tube, you have a level line, whether it is horizontal or vertical. Laser levels are fabulous for providing horizontal guides and are quite affordable now. Simply place the laser level in the middle of the room; then it casts a red laser beam

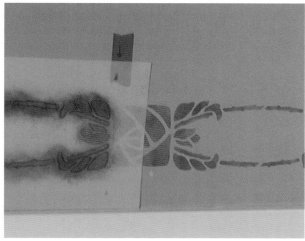

Place little pieces of masking tape on the wall or fabric underneath the stencil plate to mark the registration triangles without actually stenciling them on the project's surface, these are easily removed. A chalk line is an option to provide a horizontal guide to follow when wood trim or tile is not available.

across the wall. The better models automatically level out themselves, and the cheaper models have to be manually adjusted, but it's easy. You can refer back to the straight level, keeping it close at hand and leveling the stencil plate each time you move it. For smaller areas this is acceptable, but frankly I find it to be more work than necessary.

Another option is the good old chalk line. This method, used by every contractor at one point or another, provides an excellent horizontal guide, especially over longer distances. To give you a nice level line, there is a little device called a line level that slips over the chalk line string. Since snapping a chalk line is much easier when you have two people doing it, consider finding someone to help who is familiar with the process, espe-

duplicate a piece of the stencil image to use as a registration mark. Personally, I like working with the triangles and here's the reason why. Occasionally, you may want to lay out the stencil design ahead of time to see how it is actually going to fit on your wall or curtain. By placing little pieces of masking tape underneath the stencil plate on the wall or fabric, you can mark the registration triangles and lay out the stencil without actually stenciling any part of the design (or the registration marks for that matter) on the surface you will be painting. Then when you are ready to go for it, just line the stencil plate on the triangles. If you had used the masking tape with a piece of the design for the registration, you would have to lift the stencil plate and remove the tape before

- - - - -

It is always a good idea to use drop cloths as a precautionary measure.

- - - - -

cially if you are not. Hold the line tight against the surface on both ends and then pull it back, like the string on a bow, and let it snap back. This will lay a straight line of chalk dust against the surface. Chalk dust comes in several colors so snap the line using a color close to the wall color; remove it with a dry cloth after the stencil paint has dried. A slightly damp cloth may be used to remove any remaining residue, if necessary.

Another thing to become familiar with is stencil registration. The majority of stencils on the market today feature little cutout triangles in the corners of the stencil plate to aid in realigning the stencil. These triangles are called registration marks. Sometimes stencil designs will actually

you could actually stencil the image.

These registration marks not only help you with your vertical alignment, but the distance between the marks is also what is called the length of repeat, essentially the length of the stencil design. This length can be beneficial in laying out your design. Some stencils require that you know how many times you will be moving the stencil plate along the wall in order to lay them out, so keep this phrase in mind as we move along with the layout of the various types of stencil designs.

It is always a good idea to use drop cloths as a precautionary measure. Accidents are never planned. Nobody plans on dropping a palette or stencil brush loaded with fresh paint on new carpet.

Some other items you will want to keep on hand: paper for samples, masking tape, a level, a tape measure or ruler, and paper towels. A chalk line, plumb bob and mineral spirits will come in handy also.

I remember one job at a casino in Michigan. I was stenciling some vaulted coves about 30 feet up on a scissors lift when I heard another painter on the job loudly cursing from a nearby room. He was on a ladder when the paint jar to his sprayer unexpectedly came loose and dropped like a paint grenade on the brand-new carpet below. Believe me, it was ugly. It splattered everywhere. Eventually they did get it cleaned up, but what a hassle. I don't want you to experience such a catastrophe in your own home, so take my advice and place a drop cloth under your working area, even if it is just an old sheet from a garage sale. You will thank me later should your project encounter any mishaps.

Have some masking tape handy to place under the registration triangles so you won't have to paint little triangles all over the wall or curtain. Now, if you think it would be cool to have this additional detail added to your stencil design, that's up to you, but personally I prefer the tape method. You will have to remove all those pieces of tape after you move your stencil plate, but this is really not much of a drawback. You can also mark the triangles with a piece of chalk (no tape necessarily needed), but I find it is too easy for the chalk to accidentally smudge off and cause you to lose the registration. Then you must go back and remove all the chalked marks with a rag. Again, I like using the tape method. I rip off lots of small pieces and adhere them to an arm or pant leg. It may look funny, but they are handy and easy to get to. There are several types of low-tack painters' tape on the market today; the darker blue ones are great for taping your brushes but it can be hard to see the registration triangles when you paint them on it. Unless the wall has been recently painted, regular masking tape works fine for the registration marks.

It's also handy to have a pen or pencil to mark with or make notes, a tape measure, and a calculator, as well as the paper samples of the stencil you are going to be using. Don't forget some paper towels or rags for keeping your hands clean. If you are going to be stenciling above your head, obviously you'll need something to stand on. There are plenty of step stools and ladders to choose from, but here's another tip. Having to work off of the typical narrow ladder steps can be hard on your feet, so if you have the option of using a stepstool or ladder with wider steps, it will be more comfortable. It may be a little heavier, but it's worth it. Setting up a plank between two ladders is handy

but requires a lot more effort to move, so examine your situation. If you are doing a lot of stenciling, you may consider a more comfortable option, but if this is a small job, use whatever is convenient and handy.

Since Arts and Crafts stenciling has a variety of styles, the layout can vary between them as well, so refer to the type of design with which you will be working. If you are unsure about what style you will be working with, refer back to Chapter 1 where those differences are discussed.

– – – – –

Dominator vs. the Chain Link Gang

Although both Dominant and Chain Link stencils are referred to as border designs, they are laid out a bit differently. With Chain Link designs,

Running along the top of the ceiling, with or without wood trim, is the most common area for stencils. Since there are really no restrictions, the design has numerous possibilities.

When a picture rail is the only trim on the wall, the stencil may be placed above or below it. The frieze should be painted the same color as the ceiling and the design should incorporate the color from the wall on the other side of the rail to tie everything harmoniously together. The stencil does not necessarily have to fill the frieze area, but it is more aesthetically pleasing if it is a little smaller or larger than exactly half the width.

A frieze area bordered by wood trim on both sides is an excellent candidate for a stencil design capable of filling the area. The basic rule of thumb is that the design should be between 3 and 5 inches shorter than the height of the frieze.

you can basically start in the least dominant corner of the room and run with it. When you get back to the corner where you started, if it doesn't match, so what? If you were using a wallpaper border it probably wouldn't match either. The thing is, these stencils are often busy in themselves, so most likely only you will be the one who is going to notice. You can try to make the final corner come out perfectly by subtracting part or adding a chunk of the design, but to be honest, if this is a first-time project and you don't want to go to the extra work, don't bother. How many stencil books will tell you that? When people walk into your stenciled room, they are going to notice how beautiful your work is, not if the corners are absolutely perfect. If they do mention the corners, then just don't ever ask them back again.

With Dominant stencils, you want the dominant image to end up the same distance from the corners on whichever wall you are working on. Originally, these stencils were a bit more compli-

cated to lay out. The dominant images were individually placed on each wall, balancing out the design to complement the individual plane being worked on. The less significant images, usually some type of bar design that was easy to adjust in length, were lengthened or shortened as needed to fill in between the dominant parts. Feel free to spend the extra time and effort necessary to lay out a dominant stencil in this matter if you really wish. However, I'll share a simple trick that provides a satisfactory outcome with much less effort.

First, find the center of each wall you will be working on and mark it with a pencil line on a piece of masking tape. Keep track of the length of the wall, as you will need to divide this measurement by the length of repeat so you will know how many times to move the stencil plate. Remember the registration marks? The distance between them is the length of the design or repeat. Say your wall is 10 feet long and the repeat is 2 feet. Well, 10 divided by 2 makes 5, which will be the

With Dominant stencils, the dominant image should end up the same distance from the corners on the walls running parallel to each other. You can decide if you want the images to continue to remain the same distance apart in the corner as the rest of the pattern (as in this photo) or if you want to have the images end up equal distance from the corner on both sides. Use your paper samples and number of repeats per wall to help you decide what you like best in your situation.

number of times you will be applying the stencil to that particular wall. So here is the secret: if you have an odd number of repeats, center the dominant image on the center point of the wall and work out in both directions; if you have an even number, place the center of the less significant part (often this is some type of bar design) on the center point of the wall and work out in both directions. If you are going to stencil in the corners, the bars or simpler image will be easier to paint than the dominant portion. With this technique, it is easy to arrange to have the dominant portion of the design end up equal distances from the corner (on that particular wall anyway).

If you are concerned at all with this coming out right, lay out the design on the wall first, using the masking tape and registration triangles, before you start painting the stencil on the wall. It is much easier to remove a piece of tape and relocate the registration marks than it is to wipe off or paint over a stencil you have mistakenly placed on a wall. I know because I have experienced this personally. It may just be a coat of paint, but why paint more than you have to? To this day (and after that embarrassing situation on a job site) I always lay out dominant stencils with tape and triangles before I start stenciling. The minimal extra effort is worth the peace of mind, for I can never be sure which day my little hamster is going to jump off the wheel that powers my brain, causing my math calculations to be off.

See Spot Stencil

There are two types of Spot stencils actually. Besides the Spot, there is the Panel stencil. There isn't a lot to go into regarding either of these particular designs. After all, we are talking about stenciling just a piece of design, not a long border run with vertical alignment and corner matching. One of the easiest ways to deal with the layout of these stencils is to trust your eye, and then verify it. If you feel more comfortable working with numbers, fine. Either way, keep a ruler handy.

When stenciling a pillow with a single image, you'll probably want it centered on the pillow. Lay the unpainted stencil on the pillow, using your eye to center it, then measure the distance from all sides to make sure they are the same. The naked eye is somewhat forgiving, and it will not detect being off an eighth of an inch or less, but you will want to make adjustments if it is off by more than that. If you are finding you are not very accurate using your eye as a guideline, perhaps you should go back to a mathematical approach.

In that case, use a ruler to find the exact center of the pillow. Measure along the top and bottom of the pillow to find the center points. Place a small piece of masking tape at these center points and draw a vertical line on the tape where this occurs. Do the same with the sides of the pillow,

Paper samples will be beneficial in helping you figure out the exact placement of the design.

When using a Spot stencil on the wall, have the design the same distance from each corner and place another pattern or so along the wall to balance out the design. Use your paper samples to help give you ideas on placement. Tape them on the wall for quick visuals that are easily changed.

drawing a horizontal line at the center point. Think of it as crosshairs on the pillow. Now, measure the stencil image the same way and mark the center points with tape on the stencil plate. By aligning the stencil tape marks with the pillow tape marks, the design will be perfectly centered.

If you are using a Spot stencil on the wall, make sure the design is the same distance from each corner. Most likely you will want to place another pattern along the wall to balance out the design. For this, rely on your eyes to measure. First, stencil several samples of the design on paper and then, using your eye to guide you, tape them to the wall where you think they should go. Step back and see what they look like. Do you like it? Should you add another or take one out? If you like what you see, get out your tape measure and check the distance between them, making small

adjustments here and there to make sure they are spaced evenly. Make sure the images are the same in each corner and the other balancing images are equal distance from each other. You can repeat a Spot stencil to create a border if you so desire. But since most Spot or Panel stencils do not have registration marks (since most would not need vertical alignment as a border does), you may want to create your own registration marks on the stencil to suit your needs, once again using marks on masking tape.

A Panel stencil is similar to a Spot stencil and was designed to fit in areas like the elongated wood-trimmed panel areas in a bungalow dining room. As one might imagine, these stencils are usually quite easy to adjust to whatever length is required. And here, once again, the paper samples will be beneficial in helping you figure out the exact placement of the design.

A Spot stencil can be used in a panel area, placing the image at the top of the panel; a Panel stencil can be used like a spot design on an area of a wall or curtain. So when it comes to laying out these stencils, the techniques are similar as well. Let your eye and your paper samples initially guide you and keep a ruler handy, just in case.

How to Avoid Getting Cornered

You have practiced on paper and learned how to handle the brushes and paints you've selected, and as you make your way down the wall, you are thinking to yourself that stenciling is a piece of cake. But then it happens. You look up and see the corner approaching. Small beads of sweat start forming on your forehead and panic sets in. Well, before you totally freak out and fall off your ladder, here are some hints to help you regain your corner composure.

First, remember that it is just a corner. Earlier, I pointed out that what people are really going to notice about your stenciling is the majority of your beautiful work. I doubt they are going to scrutinize the corners. However, to make you feel more at ease, I am offering a couple of options. When I began decorative painting, I couldn't believe how many stencil books advise to fade in and out of the corner. I guess this was because they didn't know how to stencil corners or they couldn't come

up with any better solutions. I once worked with a professional painter on a job who used this technique and it looked like he didn't know how to get into the corner. At the end of the night, I went around and fixed all the corners because I knew my name would be associated with the job too. Believe me, fading in and out of corners is not a great solution.

I won't lie—corners are hard. There always seems to be globs of plaster causing lumps and bumps that refuse to be painted easily, the stencil never wants to fit in smoothly, and you almost always risk damaging it. But there are solutions.

The first solution feels almost like cheating, but it is a good form of cheating. I call it the tape method. Whether you are working with a Dominant or Chain Link stencil, this is a good alternative for dealing with corners, especially if you are a beginner. Masking tape comes in several sizes and sometimes it won't really make much of a difference if you are using 1/2-inch or 3/4-inch tape. If you are following some kind of trim or tile, then consider this extra step to make the layout look more balanced.

All stencil plates have extra material that borders the actual cutout design, and it usually runs somewhere around 1 inch. Examine the stencil plate you are using and measure the distance from the largest opening to the end of the plate to determine this measurement. Then divide that number in half and choose a roll of masking tape that size (if the extra material is 1 inch you will be using a roll of 1/2-inch tape).

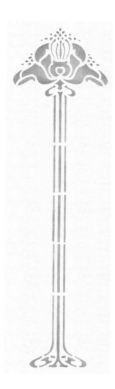

Above: *A Panel stencil is similar to a Spot stencil and was designed to fit in areas like the elongated wood-trimmed panel areas in a bungalow dining room. These stencils are usually quite easy to adjust to whatever length is required.*

Facing: *A Spot stencil can be used in a panel area, placing the image at the top of the panel (like the teapot illustration), and a Panel stencil can be used like a Spot design on an area of wall or curtain.*

Left: *Take two pieces of tape longer than the width of the stencil and run them vertically on each side of the inside corner of the wall, starting at the horizontal line. A chalk line was snapped to provide the horizontal guide.*

Below: *Bend the stencil into the corner, pushing it lightly around and realigning it on the horizontal guide on the other side. Continue stenciling up to the tape and actually stencil some overlap onto the masking tape.*

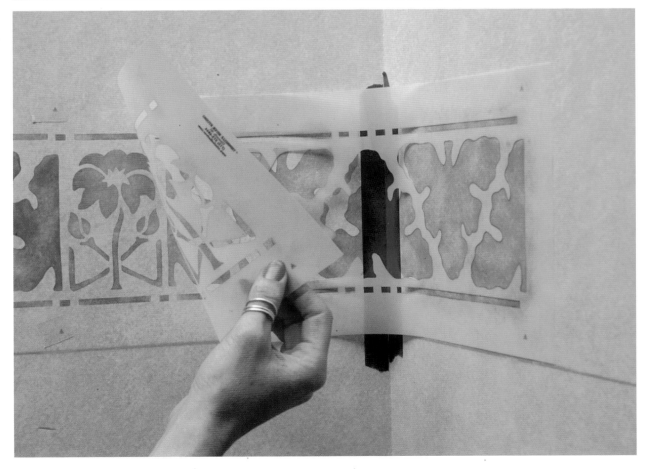

When finished, pull off the masking tape. The corners will have sharp crisp edges similar to a picture frame matte.

Take two pieces of tape longer than the width of the stencil and run them vertically on each side of the inside corner of your wall, starting at the horizontal guide. Do this with all the inside corners in the room. When you approach the corner, bend the stencil into the corner, pushing it lightly around (you don't have to cram it perfectly into the corner) and realign it on the horizontal guide on the other side. Continue stenciling up to the tape and actually stencil some overlap onto the masking tape (although you do not actually stencil the corner, you do want to stencil about 1/4 inch of the tape on both sides of the corner). When finished, pull off the masking tape. Your corners will have sharp, crisp edges, similar to a picture frame mat, especially if you have been following trim, since the corner distance will equal the distance the image is from the woodwork or tile. Because each corner has the same crisp appearance, it looks finished and appropriate. If the room has both inside and outside corners, and even though outside corners are usually easy to stencil, you may want to use tape on all the corners to keep things uniform. You decide.

After completing all the easier flat wall portions, you can take on the corners using a clean stencil plate. Here the home-owner tackles the corners after finishing all other areas of the room.

Perhaps you find the Dominant bars of the stencil you are working with hardly a hurdle. Maybe you simply want to take on the corners full speed ahead. I'll share some helpful hints to make the task a bit less daunting.

As I mentioned before, corners are tough. It is as if they were possessed by some bad juju. But there are ways to avoid the curse. First, stencil them last. When you come to a corner, place a piece of paper behind the stencil plate so you won't mark up the wall with excess paint from the stencil as you cram the plate into the corner. You will have to cram it—although not quite as severely as when you actually stencil the corner. This time around, you are just looking to get the plate realigned on the horizontal guide so you can get the registration marks. Once you get the registration down, lift the stencil, remove the paper and

continue stenciling on the other side of the corner. Remember, you are not actually stenciling the corner at this point; although if you wish, you can stencil a portion of the stencil plate, just leave out the image that will appear in the corner. Do this with each inside corner you come to. Outside corners are no big deal; just let the excess stencil plate hang loose as you stencil each side of the wall.

After you have completed all the easy parts of the walls, you can now tackle the corners. Start by cleaning the stencil plate and remove all paint from it. You will only be stenciling a portion of the design now so you don't need excess paint everywhere to create a mess. I highly recommend using the stencil adhesive in this situation; it helps to hold down the bridges in the corners, even though they often want to flop around. Take the clean stencil and realign it in the corner. You will have to

- - - - -

Remember, if it isn't perfect, the chances are good that you will be the only one who sees it, especially if you don't point it out to everyone who comments on your stenciling.

- - - - -

cram the stencil plate in tight because it has to lay flat on the wall in order to get a crisp image. It will probably want to lie flat on one side and buckle on the other—that's fine. You will only be stenciling one side at a time anyway. Be prepared to hold the plate down in the corner with your fingers, even with the adhesive, so keep a rag handy to clean your hands. Finally, don't be surprised if the stencil brush seems a bit too big to get into the corner to stencil. All of this is normal when it comes to corners.

Often the brushes you use on the wall appear to be too large to work efficiently in the corner. After all, you probably used as big a brush as possible to make the stenciling go faster. The problem is, other types of artists' brushes usually apply the paint in a different consistency than a stencil brush and so if you use a different type of applicator, it will probably be apparent. A corner that appears darker than the rest of the stenciling is just about as obvious as the fading-in-and-out technique. The solution? Well, smaller stencil brushes certainly would work, but they often have to be pretty small. Instead, I use a stiff artist brush commonly used with oil paintings. This stiff bristle brush, when used with a stippling or pouncing technique, will apply the paint in a similar fashion as the stencil brush. Do as much as you can with the stencil brush and if you need to get in even tighter, try a tinier stencil brush or a stiffer oil

brush. Do your best at getting the area stenciled. Remember, if it isn't perfect, the chances are good that you will be the only one who sees it, especially if you don't point it out to everyone who comments on your stenciling.

Certain designs will be much harder to stencil into a corner. Images with long floppy bridges are especially tricky. Don't be surprised if, when you are finished, the stencil looks like it had a tangle with stencil-hater. Vintage stencil books told the painter to take a ruler and actually put a crease in the oil board stencils for corners, often recommending the painter have more than one stencil for this reason. No wonder the original oil-board stencil rarely survived—they were brutally abused on the job! Your modern plastic stencil may look a bit worn after dealing with corners, but most likely it will not have to go to stencil heaven like the old oil-board plates of days past. Should it need to function again down the road, I think you'll be pleasantly surprised at the outcome. Of course, when you are through with your stencil, it is up to you to determine its final outcome.

- - - - -

Skimming the Surfaces

If you ask some guy in a warehouse about stenciling, he will probably refer you to a counter where some cutout letters spelling the word FRAG-ILE sit next to a can of black spray paint. Outside of that, I think the more common place people think of stenciling is on a wall. Frieze areas along the ceiling, around chair rails or above tile in a bathroom were common places where stenciling was used during the Arts and Crafts period. But there are plenty of other surfaces appropriate for stenciling, and even walls have various surfaces to deal with. So let's expand our horizon and delve into some of these other options.

Old plaster finishes do not cause much of a problem when stenciling, and actually add another dimension to the stenciling.

If You've Been Plastered— Dealing With Textured Walls

The most frequently asked questions I get are about stenciling textured walls. "Can I do it?" Well of course you can. You can paint practically anything if you are really determined. When my brother was little, he tried painting the dog.

The point is, you can stencil just about anything. When it comes to a textured wall, there are regular textures and then there are deep cavernous textures. Old, somewhat-lumpy original plaster walls are really not much of a texture when it comes to stenciling. The same goes with what is referred to as "Orange Peel" or "Sand" finishes. Yes, there is a texture to the surface, but these are rather mild forms of textures, and though they add another dimension to the stenciling, they don't really interfere much with the stenciling process. You can pretty much stencil this type of a textured surface like it was plain old plasterboard.

There exist textures that are referred to as "Knock Down" finishes. Think of stucco on the

outside of a house and you get the idea that this kind of texture is definitely going to require a little extra effort when stenciling. Consider that only about 50 percent of your stencil plate is going to make contact with a heavy textured surface like this. But that doesn't mean it can't be stenciled.

I recommend using the stencil adhesive on walls with heavy textures, but also use masking tape as a secondary measure to help hold the stencil onto the wall. Remember, only about 50 percent of the plate is making contact with the wall. The sheer weight of the stencil can fall off the wall, therefore the masking tape is beneficial. The adhesive also helps keep the bridges down while you are stenciling.

Another problem with a highly textured wall is that it is easier to get paint under the stencil plate. To avoid this, make sure you hold the stencil brush perpendicular to the wall surface. If you treat it like an artist brush or a pencil and hold it at a 45-degree angle, the brush bristles can easily slip under the stencil plate and make contact with the 50 percent of the wall that isn't making contact with the stencil plate.

It will be hard to get edges crisp and sharp when stenciling heavy textures, so don't get overzealous about this. Instead, realize that when you step back from the wall, your eye naturally fills in the gaps and the stencil outline will appear sharper than it looks from up close. Heavy textures create stenciling that can be quite lovely, but avoid designs that have lots of small or narrow openings. Instead, stick to simpler designs that have larger cutout areas and fewer fine details.

Stenciling combined with a Tiffany finish in a Milwaukee home creates this beautiful effect, typical of Arts and Crafts stenciling.

Faux Or Faux Pas?

Another type of texture you may have to deal with on a surface is one that you can see but not necessarily feel. Today we refer to the art of decorative wall finishing as "Faux Finishing," with *faux* being French for "fake." But during the Arts and Crafts movement, they didn't try to fake the look of natural elements like making a piece of wood look like a hunk of marble. If they wanted marble, they used marble. They did use decorative finishes on walls, but the wall finishes at that time were often soft and simple for the most part—color washes, subtle ragging and wet sponge techniques. There were some wilder, more colorful effects referred to as "Tiffany" finishes that resembled art glass. Stenciling was used with all of them.

If you wish to use a decorative finish on the wall before you stencil, that's fine. It is always wise to do some extra sample boards of the wall technique you plan on using so that you can also stencil a sample on that surface before heading to your wall. Depending on what paint medium you are

using and how heavily you are applying it, you may or may not see the finish under your stenciling. Oil-based paints often show more of a watercolor appearance and so it is likely you will see some of the decorative wall finish in the stenciling. If the finish is subtle, it shouldn't make that much difference, but if you used a ragging technique with quite a bit of contrast between the wall base and glazing colors, you are likely to see some of the ragging through the stenciling. A water-based stencil paint applied in a more opaque manner will likely not show any signs of ragging. If you have concerns at all about how your stenciling will look over a decorative wall finish, do sample boards from start to finish before you even put on the wall finish. Touching up decorative wall finishes is difficult, so it is best to do the samples ahead of time to see if you like the effect. Then again, it is just a coat of paint—you can always paint the whole thing over again if necessary. Which would you rather do?

Flat Or Glossy?

One unexpected thing to watch out for is not necessarily if the paint is oil- or water-based, but

The Craftsman *published this in August 1905, but the idea behind it is just as applicable today. A forest frieze with plain plaster below allows the lower wall to be painted in an easier-to-clean finish in this children's room. This way the decorative treatment can be applied to a finish more receptive to receive it.*

rather what kind of sheen will you be working on. Flat or matte wall sheens are more porous and are very absorbent. Paints will adhere to them easily and give you more intense colors, especially when you are working with oil stencil paints. As you move up in sheen, the wall surface starts to lose its porosity. What this means is that less and less paint will stick to the surface, which also means that as you move into the glossy paint category, it is going to be harder and harder to paint. Think about it. Why do people choose gloss and semigloss paints in the first place? Because they are easy to clean. And why are they so easy to clean? Well, because dirt doesn't stick to the surface as easily. What makes you think stencil paint is going to want to stick any better?

With the fabulous advancements in paint technology and the washing ability of even eggshell fin-

ishes, I'm not sure why people use gloss paints anymore. I'm sorry if you just finished painting the bathroom last night in a semigloss, but don't fret. There is still hope for you and your stenciling. However, you will need to perform an extra step, so here are some options.

You could repaint. Now, if you haven't recently painted the wall you plan on stenciling, I advise that you do so. When stenciling, you can never be sure that there won't be a stray fingerprint to touch up, and I am guessing you would like the new paint to match the old. Therefore, make the effort to have a wall surface that has been painted within the last year or so. If the wall doesn't fall into this category, repaint with as low a sheen finish as you can tolerate.

Realize that repainting doesn't mean you have

to repaint the whole wall, but it might be a good excuse if you didn't really care for the lime green anyway. You can just repaint the area where you plan to stencil. Simply mask off a band on the wall where you'll be stenciling, obviously a little larger than the stencil image, and repaint that area in either the same color, but in a lower sheen finish or in a slightly different color with lower sheen. Taping the area off can also provide you with that

Often what you will find is that the glossier surfaces will only accept so much paint, so the stenciling will appear more muted than your paper samples. The paint will take longer to dry and also will not want to adhere as securely, so if you are a wall washer, beware of scrubbing the paint off if you use too much elbow grease, even after it has supposedly cured.

Suppose you never read this section of the

- - - - -

I always get a kick out of watching people's faces when I explain they can stencil on fabrics as well as on their walls.

- - - - -

horizontal guideline you may need as well. You could also rag or sponge this taped-off band with a flat glaze. That too, will provide you with a better surface for stenciling.

If you just can't repaint, there is another option. Mask off a band where the stenciling will go, just as if you were repainting. This time, use super-fine steel wool or sandpaper and lightly sand over the area to slightly rough up the surface. Do not use a lot of pressure or you will go through the paint layer. All you want to do is give the surface some tooth for the paint to stick to. Most likely you will see an obvious change on the paint surface, but by masking off the area the sheen change will appear as a band or a border rather than as random scribble marks. Make sure you wipe off the dusty residue before you stencil.

If you are simply not interested in any of the previous options, there is one more thing to try. Paint a couple of pieces of poster board with two coats of the same paint that is currently on the wall. When it is dry, stencil that surface to see the result without actually stenciling on the wall.

book and have already gone ahead and stenciled over the glossy surface and now are returning in search of solutions or guidance as to why it doesn't seem to be drying. There are aerosol quick drying top coats that may help, but make sure it is compatible with the stencil paint and remember to mask off the area in case it changes the sheen. Otherwise I'm afraid, you'll have to live with it. Really. Yes, it is not going to be as durable, so don't wash it abusively. Perhaps the more muted effect will start to grow on you. If it does bother you, paint over it. As a precautionary measure, give it a light sanding, then tack and prime it before you repaint, just to ensure you don't create any more unnecessary problems. Next time, sand before you stencil instead of after.

- - - - -

It's a Material Thing

I always get a kick out of watching people's faces when I explain they can stencil on fabrics as well as their walls. It's as if I just told them I have a cat that can do tricks. They want to consider this; after all everyone knows that cats only do what they want when they want, so surely this would be exceptional. Still they want to see it in person. So I show them various forms of stenciled fabrics from linens to sheers to velvets. Their eyes light up as their imaginations crank into high gear.

The truth is that fabrics were widely stenciled during the Arts and Crafts movement. Influential characters of the period like Gustav Stickley encouraged homeowners to participate in the decorative arts of their homes and stenciling was a wonderful way for them to do it, whether it was used on walls or fabrics. Table linens, pillows, curtains and portieres as well as more "womanly" items like pincushions, laundry bags and clothing accessories were viable options. Stenciling was everywhere in the modest little bungalow.

The homeowner could purchase a precut sten-cil alone or as a complete stencil kit with paints and brushes. They could cut their own design, choosing a pattern from one of the current magazines at the time or creating their own. Whatever the case might be, fabrics were definitely a part of stenciling throughout the home. These stenciled fabrics often were further embellished with embroidery, the amount dependent upon the time and talent of the homeowner. A simple stem stitch could have outlined a stenciled leaf or a more complicated stitch could have been used to fill in an area. It just depended on what the artist wanted to do. That was the beauty of it.

Stenciling fabrics is a bit different than stenciling paper samples or drywall. As with most projects, it is wise to experiment on a sample piece of similar fabric before heading off to stencil the curtains. Although most materials are quite suitable for stenciling, there are a few to avoid. Heavy textured fabrics absorb the paint unevenly, but if you are

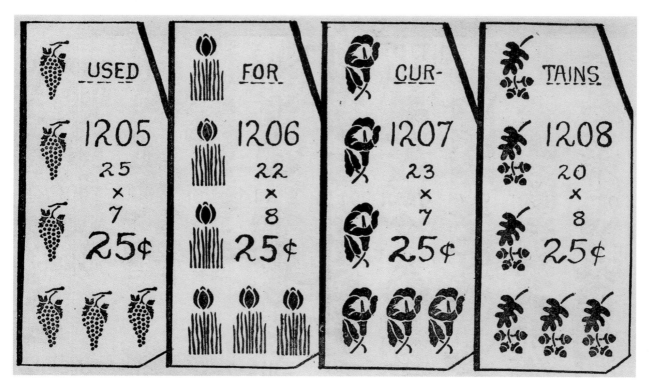

Above: *Stencils for curtains from a vintage catalog.*

Facing: *Stenciling a curtain in 1908.*

A vintage example of a stenciled blouse using the upper stencils on the following page.

working in one color, it can give another dimension to your work. Wools contain natural oil that can prevent the paint from adhering and water-repellent fabrics are likely to repel the paint as well. Fabrics like velvet and chiffon are not good choices for beginning stencilers, but both materials are quite spectacular when stenciled.

The first thing to do before stenciling on fabric is to wash the fabric in order to remove any sizing or treatments applied to it. Don't use a fabric softener or bleach, as they can inhibit paint adhesion. Napkins and tablecloths may be treated with stain retardants and should be washed several times before stenciling, so check the labels. Most fabrics will need to be pressed after washing (no starch) so the material will lay flat during stenciling. If you plan on using an oil-based paint, do not work with fabrics that are "dry clean only" as the solvents used in the cleaning process can actually remove the paint.

The paper samples you made will help you with your color selection, and in the case of working with fabrics, they can really help you with the placement of your design. Usually some part of the design will center on the center point of the fabric, along the edge of a table runner or curtain for example. An easy way to find the center of a piece of material is to fold the fabric in half and mark it somehow by creasing it or marking it with dressmakers chalk. You could also place a piece of low-tack tape near the center and mark the center point on the tape with a pencil or pen. Don't mark with a pencil directly on the fabric; it can be surprisingly difficult to remove, even when washed.

Assemble all your project ingredients together before you start. Stopping to retrieve a forgotten item is an annoying delay when you are stenciling. As with stenciling a wall, you will need to decide on a paint medium once again. Personally, I like using the solid oil-based paints, like Shiva Paintstiks or Delta Crème Paints, because the blending and shading effects achieved with them are superior. Since they are oil-based, they dry to a soft flexible finish. Water-based textile paints are commonly used, and are certainly an option, but I find they are not as easy to work with, nor do they provide the same beautiful effects as the oil-based paint. I personally do not care for the crispy stiff feeling that the majority of dried acrylics leave on fabric.

I highly recommend using a repositionable stencil adhesive when working on fabrics. It allows the stencil plate to adhere to the surface of the fabric, and prevents the slippery plastic stencil from sliding all over the place without leaving any residue. If you are working on heavier fabrics and you are not worrying about paint bleeding through, you can also spray the shiny side of a poster board with the adhesive, and allow it to set up for a couple of minutes. Then lay the material on top, smoothing out the wrinkles. This will hold the fabric tight and also keep it from shifting. Now lay the stencil on top and the fabric is sandwiched between the stencil and the ridged poster board, unable to escape on its own. As long as you allow the adhesive to dry before making contact with your fabric, it should not leave any residue and makes the job easier.

If you don't use the poster board technique, still smooth the fabric out on top of a hard, clean surface. You may want to tape the edges down with a low tack tape to hold the fabric secure. If you are working with a fairly stiff fabric like canvas or cotton velvet, you may not need to take this extra step. If you choose a fabric that is light or has a loose weave, place paper towels or blank newspaper underneath the fabric, as the paint is likely to bleed through. You will still want to use the adhesive on the back of the stencil plate, but don't bother with the poster board. If you encounter the paint bleeding through, you will be having to change the paper underneath each time you need to move the stencil plate.

Remember you will need a separate brush for each color in the stencil. Taping the brushes is beneficial when working with fabrics as it allows you more control over the bristles (see page 59 on taping brushes). Note that fabrics generally use more paint than a hard wall

Two sets of period blouse stencils. The yoke stencil measured about 6 1/2 inches whereas the cuff design was only 3 inches. The smallest design could be used down the sleeve to link the two together.

Fine details are brought out when stenciled fabrics are enhanced with embroidery.

does. Apply the paint by gently working it through the openings, caressing it into the fibers in a circular motion. Start with a light coat and increase the pressure to darken an area. Pulling the brush from the outside of the stencil opening towards the center helps define the edges. Keep in mind that the fabric will want to absorb more paint than you might think, so error on the side of using less paint to start with. With the oil-based mediums, you can always go back and add a little more paint if necessary. With the water-based, what you put down the first time is pretty much what you are going to get, as they are definitely not as forgiving.

An important thing to remember in working with fabrics is to keep the work area clean, and especially your hands. Removing an undesired fingerprint from your beautiful table runner can be quite a challenge; it is simply better to not allow it to get there in the first place. But mistakes can happen. Should they happen on your masterpiece, try using a product called Kiss-Off or a bit of The Master's Brush Cleaner and Preserver. These products are available at most crafts and artist materials stores and work with pretty much any paint medium. Be careful about getting either of these products on an area where you would prefer the paint not be removed. When working with oil-based paint, avoid using paint thinner to remove unwanted paint as this usually causes the mistake to simply bleed into a larger spot.

When the project is completed, it should be fairly dry to the touch if you've worked with the solid oil paints. I sometimes drape the fabric over the railing in the stairwell or hang it on a clothesline. With oil, the surface is usually quite dry, so I can often stack the fabric with a piece of tissue paper or blank newsprint in between without having any problems. With water-based paints though, your fabric may remain wet for a while, so do not fold or stack your material as it finishes drying.

Heat Setting and Cleaning

Most paints require you to heat-set them to make them more durable. This is a simple proce-

*Original stenciled textiles
embellished with embroidery.*

- - - - -

*An important thing to remember in
working with fabrics is to keep the work area clean,
and especially your hands.*

- - - - -

dure using an iron. Let the paint cure for at least a few days. The longer you wait, the more permanent it will be. Set your iron for the hottest temperature recommended for the fabric you are heat-setting. With the solid oils, place a piece of wax paper over the design and iron for about 10 seconds on both sides to set the paint. If you are working with water-based paints, you can skip the wax paper, but check to see if there are any other recommendations for heat-setting your specific medium. Otherwise, heat-set in the same manner as previously mentioned. Fabrics like velvets, which can be difficult to iron, can be heat set in a commercial dryer—just let them tumble in the heat briefly. As long as you put them in dry, not wet, you shouldn't have a problem with them shrinking.

In regards to cleaning, don't dry clean anything stenciled with oils. But after the fabric is heat-set, you can certainly wash it. Yes, you can throw it in the washing machine, but keep in mind that just like any pair of blue jeans, if you subject your stenciling to the agitation of a machine, it will fade eventually.

There are several things you can do to clean stenciled fabric and prevent wear and tear.

▪ Treat it like a delicate. Use cold water, mild soap, and minimal cool tumbling if needed.

■ Wash it in a pillowcase to help protect it from the abrasion of bumping into other items in the wash.

■ Toss it in a dryer with a wet terrycloth towel. A lot of items like curtains and pillows don't actually get that dirty; they simply get dusty. A tumble in a cool dryer with a wet towel will lift the dust from its surface. This might at least help limit the amount of washing necessary.

■ Finally, after the finished piece is dry and heat-set, consider spraying it with a fabric protector like Scotchgard, applied in several light mistings. This makes minor cleanings with a damp rag easier, but test it on your fabric sample before spraying all your curtains, just in case.

Wood You or Wood You Knot? Furniture and Floors

Although furniture and floors were not widely stenciled during the Arts and Crafts movement, there were times when someone simply wanted something a little different. The same is true today. If this appeals to you, here are some tips.

When it comes to floors, keep in mind you are going to want a fairly simple strong design like

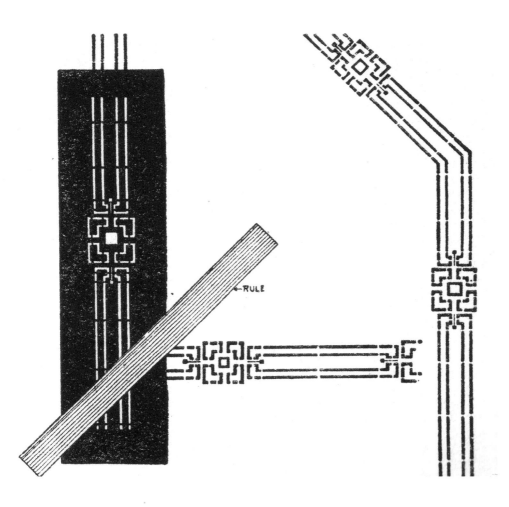

Geometric patterns work well for floors, as they are easy to adapt to corners. The design should be the same distance from the baseboard all around the room, disregarding small discrepancies.

geometric stencils that consist of bars, squares or triangles. The size will be determined more or less by the size of the room. Even if the pattern comes with a matching corner piece, you will still have to do some planning in order to make it fit in the room, so have your tape measure and calculator handy. The design should be the same distance from the baseboard all around the room, disregarding small discrepancies.

Painted surfaces provide the best surface for stenciling. However, since floors take a lot of abuse, you may find that a good portion of paint specified for floors will be nonporous and there-

stenciling will most likely be varnished and still need to be given some tooth for the paint to adhere. Certainly any old wax will need to be removed as well.

Painting the cabinet doors that adorn your bungalow kitchen with the 1950s or '60s "renovation" is a great option in making your kitchen look more original without the expense of replacing them. Choose paint with a lower sheen for stenciling and if you want the surface more durable for cleaning, use a satin or semigloss compatible topcoat. I highly recommend using an aerosol for the initial application of the top-

– – – – –

Painting the cabinet doors that adorn your bungalow kitchen with the 1950s or '60s "renovation" is a great option in making your kitchen look more original without the expense of replacing them.

– – – – –

fore may not want to let your stencil paint adhere to it very well. Look for an option that has a flatter finish or consider the techniques for roughing up glossier surfaces (page 91). A technique used during this period of stenciling was to paint the floor with a border slightly darker than the center area. Then the stenciling would be placed on the lighter inside surface. This would give the floor more of a rug appearance or actually make a nice backdrop for a rug. If you want to work on an unpainted wood floor, consider painting the stencil in a similar contrasting color so as to look like inlaid wood, such as a fumed oak color over a light oak floor. Old floors have old finishes so the area you plan on

coat to set the stencil paint. After this dries, you can brush on a heavier protective layer. Talk to a reputable paint dealer in your area to make sure that what you purchase for the protective layers is compatible with the type of paint you used for stenciling. There have been many improvements in paint mediums over the years and you might be surprised at how friendly the old oil and water mediums have become. I cannot stress enough how important it is to do a sample—complete from sanding to topcoat—to see if any of the finishes need to be changed before you start on the cabinets or the floor.

I understand there may be times when you just don't have an extra piece of old maple flooring hanging around in the basement to do a sample on. Fake it. Find a piece of salvage flooring or wood; get a board with a similar finish to the kitchen cabinets. The point is to do the process, from preparing the original finish to applying the final protective layer. Sure it is going to be extra work. But consider how much work it would be to strip all the paint off your project because it blistered or you simply didn't like the way it turned out. If you decide to skip the sample, good luck. Take your chances and deal with the consequences.

It's Really Not That Technical

In case you haven't noticed by now, I am not a huge fan of stenciling with water-based paints. Sure, they have their place in time (every couple of centuries, like 1780 and 1980; maybe I'll appreciate them in the year 2180). As I see what

Start by applying a very light coat of paint over the whole area. It can look a little mottled and doesn't have to be totally solid in appearance. Wherever you want the stencil to appear darker, increase the pressure you are using to stencil. Less paint and more pressure will achieve better results.

can be done with the oil-based paint mediums, I simply cannot understand why anyone would want to work with anything else unless they have to.

The craftsman of the Arts and Crafts movement certainly appreciated the benefits and capabilities of oils as well; this is evident by the numerous references I have found throughout my vintage decorative painting library. Although they certainly did not have the latex paint medium of today, there were still plenty of water-based paint mediums. Back then, the decorative painter realized how much more could be achieved with oil.

Today, our fear and hatred of stinky oil paints has the decorative painting business fussing over how to get their water-based paints to perform like the oil glazes of yesteryear. They add paint-drying extenders, attempting to delay the time it takes for a water-based glaze to dry or set up. But these mediums still really can't compete, even if they are more appealing to the public to use. They just are not the same and this is why it is so much harder to try and get a water-based wash finish to truly

The image will often appear lighter than it actually is when you are looking at it through a stencil plate. Check out the intensity by lifting one edge, take a peek and let the plate fall back in place. Don't lift the whole stencil plate off the surface; it can be a bit of a challenge getting it exactly right again.

look like an oil-based wash finish originally done in 1915. So why should it be any different with stencil paints?

If oils worked so well back then, why shouldn't they be used today (My point exactly!)? Especially since the development of the so-called "dry brush" or "crème" paints; which are simply oil-based paints in a solid form. The advantage over this oil-paint medium is that it is dryer. Therefore the undesirable bleed or shadow around the stencil image that can be a problem with an oilier medium, especially on fabrics when applied heavily, is a much less significant risk. This means you too can achieve the beautiful blending and shading techniques that the artists of old created, only with a lot less headache. Isn't technology great?

A Shady Deal to Be Had

If you were going to a fine arts college, it would take a while to graduate from working with plain black drawing pencils and charcoal to working with color. It's because you need to first realize what using one color can do before becoming amazed by what you can do when working with an abundance of hues.

Shading is the first basic step to creating beautiful stencil work and it's really easy. Most stencil guides out there focus on acrylics and patterns like apples when it comes to shading. Either the paint is applied solidly so that no shading is

Shading is the first basic step to creating beautiful stencil work and it's really easy.

All of the following techniques are done with an oil-based paint medium called a Paintstik. Once again, this is an oil paint in a solid form, about the consistency of lipstick. They are very easy to use, not nearly as messy to work with as most water-based paints and they go an incredibly long way. In an average room, with an average design, you will be lucky to go through even half an inch of any color stick you are using in your stencil. And since they reseal themselves in about 24 to 48 hours, they keep for a very long time; much longer than any little bottle of acrylic paint from your local craft mart.

apparent, or the paint on the outside of the apple is applied dark and then the color is faded out as it approaches the center. The problem with this technique is that the center is often faded out so much that the color can hardly be seen. It is a rudimentary lesson in shading, but I have never seen an apple that really looks like that. Although you can try to make the stenciling look as if light is being reflected off the apple, it is not necessary. Lovely effects can be achieved without doing so and without aiming at deception. You are not trying to paint some Dutch Old Master's rose here, so don't try to make it look like one. Instead, aim for creating some beautiful stenciling and use your shading for highlights and lowlights, not a goofy-looking apple.

To start with, load just a little paint on your brush. When you use oils, you can always add another layer to intensify the color. Try to discover a nice balance between how much paint is on the brush and how much pressure is being applied to the stencil. Remember, less paint/more pressure will achieve better results.

Start by applying a light coat of paint over the whole area. It can look a little mottled and it does not have to be totally solid in appearance. Realize that what you see through the stencil openings can be quite deceiving as the stencil plate starts

to accumulate paint residue. It will appear lighter than it actually is, so make sure you look under the plate and check out the intensity of the paint on the wall, especially when you start working on your samples in the beginning of your project. Simply lift one edge, take a peek and let the plate fall back in place. Don't lift the whole stencil plate off the surface or it will be difficult getting it back in place exactly.

Wherever you want the stencil to appear darker, increase the pressure. If this doesn't work well enough, then apply a little more paint to the brush, but start with simply pushing a little harder. Again, check what the stencil

There are two basic ways to blend colors together. One way allows the colors to remain truer, while the other way alters the colors by layering.

Start by applying color #1 about halfway into the stencil opening, leaving the second half unpainted.

really looks like by lifting the edge of the plate. If you want it a bit darker in some areas, let the stencil fall back into place and add another layer of paint with more pressure or with a little more paint.

When you first start experimenting with this technique on paper, try to see how much variation you can achieve within your design simply by using only one color. You will be pleasantly amazed at what just a single color is capable of.

Creating a Union with Color— The Bond of Blending

Now that you have a little experience in shading, let's have a little fun with blending. Although

Next, fill in the unpainted half with color #2; where the two colors form a seam, take your brush and very lightly pull the two colors into each other, softening the transition.

you can attempt these blending techniques with a water-based medium, it will be more difficult and the results will not be the same. You will have to work much more quickly or risk having the paint set up too fast, which will cause problems when blending and shading.

There are two ways to blend and shade colors together. The first method allows the two colors to remain truer and actually creates a third color where they meet and are blended. The second method requires actually altering one of the two

colors by layering the second color on top. This method works well when trying to tone down a color without having to custom mix it on a palette. I suggest experimenting with both variations of blending to get the idea. Working with two primary colors will show more contrast and variety in your experimentation.

For the first method, start by applying the first color about halfway into the stencil opening, leaving the second half unpainted. Next, fill in the unpainted half with the second color. When you

Apply the first color (or the color you want to alter) over the whole open area and shade it to the desired intensity.

get to the middle where the two colors are going to bump into each other and form a seam, take your brush and very lightly swirl it back and forth over the seam. This pulls the two colors into each other and softens the transition. You don't want to necessarily go far into either color; just smooth out the harsh stripe or seam where the two come together. You can use a third brush to do your blending if you want, or you can use either of the brushes that you just used to apply the colors. If you use one of your original brushes, keep an eye

on it to make sure it isn't picking up too much of the opposite color and making the brush muddy. With the dry oil paints, so little paint is used that you can usually remove any of the wrong color from the bristles by rubbing the end of the blending brush on a paper towel or clean lint-free rag. If you are experiencing problems with the brushes picking up too much of the wrong color, try using a separate blending brush. Also, try using less paint and attempt to keep your stencil plate cleaner as well.

Apply the second color on top of this first color. Try variations of altering the color along the edge of the design or the whole first color. Play on the sample papers to see what appeals to you and watch for muddy brushes.

The second method requires alteration of a color. First, apply the color you plan on altering over the whole opening and shade it to whatever intensity you like. Then, apply the second color on top of the first color. You may want to go over the whole first color or only a part of it. Be aware that if you applied the first color fairly heavy and you are planning on applying the second color completely over the first, you are more likely to taint the second-color brush. Be prepared to wipe it off on a towel more frequently than if you used the first method.

I often find it is a nice effect to just allow a little color to sneak into an adjoining area—just a bit. It usually adds a nice element to the design, like a touch of the green used on a flower stem to nip the base of the flower bud. You don't have to necessarily cross over a lot. A simple smidgen of color can make a world of difference. On your paper samples, try both ways and see what you think. This hint of color may add extra charm to your design without a lot of effort.

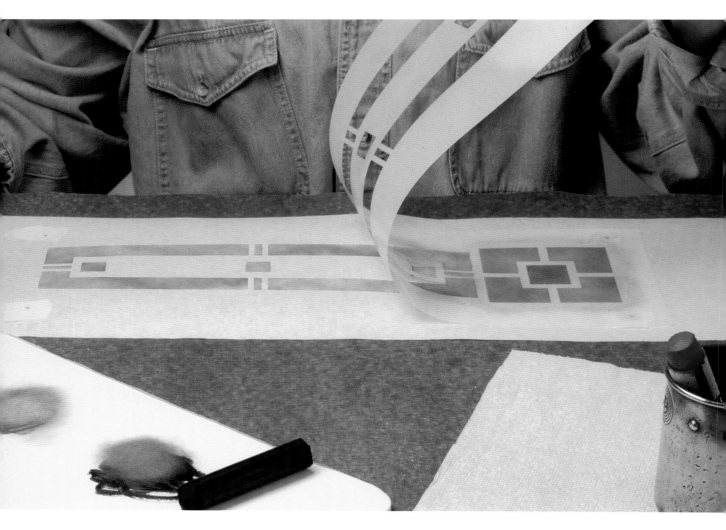

Marbling is especially attractive in the bar areas of more geometric designs, adding another dimension to an image that is often simpler.

There Is More to Marbling than Tombstones and Steaks

If you want to give your stenciling a fabulous unique look, try this cool variation of the blending technique. It is especially attractive in the bar areas of more geometric designs, adding another dimension to an image that is often simpler. When used throughout the whole design, it is also a fast technique. There is no problem with using larger brushes, so that speeds up the stenciling process. If you are struggling with the problem of which area to use a color, do a paper sample marbling the whole design with the colors you have selected. Sometimes this ends up being the perfect solution.

As with the blending, there are a couple of

The first thing you want to do is create a flow of color. Use a darker hue to establish the flow more boldly and make it easier to see. Widen the flow line by extending it on both sides.

variations to use with a marbling technique. You may find one easier or you may have a preference depending the size of your project. You can certainly experiment with your own version—make it unique to you!

Since I refer to this technique as marbling, I'll explain the main method from which you can experiment and vary. The key to this method is to not think too hard about what you are doing—that will only complicate matters. Allow your mind to relax and just have fun with this. I love

stenciling in this manner whenever I work with the bars in designs. It is such a wonderful effect and it is so easy.

When you are blending colors, it is important to look at the whole image of the design rather than at each individual cutout area. If your stencil has oak leaves with the veins of the leaves separating each leaf into lots of cutout openings, remember to still treat the leaf as a whole. Don't try shading each individual little opening; shade the image of the leaf as if there weren't any bridges or

Fill in the unpainted area with your lighter color. Make sure all the background is eventually covered. Where the two colors meet, you will once again blend the seams together.

gaps. The same goes for marbling. If there are three bars running together, treat them as if they were one large bar. In this case, see the whole design by not seeing the bridges.

First, establish a flow of color. Think of a river meandering through the woods rather than a perfect zigzag of rickrack trim. For other techniques, I recommend starting with your lightest color and progressing to the darkest one, simply because it is always easier to go darker than it is to go lighter. But in this case, I like to start with a darker hue

because it establishes the flow of color more boldly and makes it easier to see.

Once you have established a flow pattern, widen the line by extending it on both sides, letting up on the pressure so as to let the color gradually fade out. You want to have areas where you have left the background unpainted. If you have a large unpainted area, say in a corner opposite your flow pattern, you may want to put a little of the color used to establish the flow in that location, just to keep some unity. Once again, this is a

Make the marbling even a little more unique by adding a third darker color. Apply it randomly and sparsely.

good example of how paper samples can help you determine what you like and don't like.

After this is completed, fill in the unpainted areas with the lighter color. Make sure all the background is eventually covered. Here too, you can create some shading within the areas where your second color is going. Where the two colors meet, blend the seams together. Start by using pressure rather than more paint at first. Allow the two colors to gently caress each other and soften the transition between the two.

To make the marbling even more cool, I like to add a third darker color, applying it randomly and sparsely. Experiment with the paper samples to see what appeals to you most. Also try mottling the colors in a more random or spotty pattern. This can be quite nice in smaller areas where establishing a flow can be a bit of a challenge. The key is to just have fun with it and create unique effects, but don't get so creative that you won't be able to duplicate it again when you have to move your stencil plate. ■

As You Go:
Keeping an Eye on Things

ongratulations! You're finally stenciling! Aren't you glad you spent all that time reading and practicing on paper ahead of time? Think of all those little glitches and even some major mistakes you avoided. Go ahead and take pride in the fabulous work of art you are now creating. If you feel like there is still a little room left in your brain to learn something, or if you think you can handle a few more reminders, here are some last useful tidbits regarding stenciling.

No matter what the stencil is made of or which paint medium you decide to go with, there are some tips to pay attention to as you stencil away.

If you are noticing the appearance of fuzzy lines around your design rather than sharp crisp edges, you probably have too much paint on your stencil brush and it is creeping under the stencil plate. Check the stencil and brushes because they may need a slight cleaning. Wipe the brushes on a fresh paper towel, twisting any excess paint off the sides. For the stencil plate, lay it on a clean piece of paper, like freezer wrap or blank newsprint, and gently wipe it with a paper towel. If you are using oils, you should be able to easily wipe most of excess paint residue from the stencil plate. If you are using acrylics, you will need to moisten the towel with water. Remember this last type of medium likes to attach itself to the plate and is more reluctant to remove. It may be easier to try to keep the stencil plate as clean as possible while you are working by pulling the excess paint off the plate and into the openings as you stencil. Remember to follow the stencil bridges as you wipe to avoid causing damage to the plate.

If you are working with the stencil adhesive, recoat when the stencil starts to lose its tack or spot spray a bridge that might be starting to lift and catch on your brush. Remember, it is best to use a light coat of adhesive; stay away from squirting the stencil plate like a hornet nest with raid. Too many heavy coats will only cause problems.

When working with a multiple overlay stencil, or any time you need to store the stencil for a while before finishing the job, lay the adhesive side of the plate on wax paper (or the waxy shiny side of freezer wrap) rather than on paper. When the

Sometimes to make a corner fit, you will need to add an extra piece of your stencil design. Use your paper sample to help decide your best option.

adhesive is still quite tacky, it can stick to the paper and pull some of the fibers with it upon removal. Wax paper eliminates this problem. You can also lay the plate with the painted side down, as long as you are not stacking a bunch of layers on top of each other; but you don't want to do this for long periods of time as the adhesive will pick up dust and other floating particles that pass by it.

It is important to make sure you check how the work is going by frequently stepping back and examining your progress. This will allow you to keep your colors fairly even and let you catch any necessary changes that might need to be made. Some variation in the color is good. After all, you do want your stenciling to look like it is

hand-painted. Remember, however, that drastic differences diminish the beauty.

- - - - -

Making It Fit: The Flexibility of Stenciling

Once again, the hardest part of stenciling is dealing with corners and making the stencil fit. Even if you have carefully measured and planned to have five exact repeats of the stencil on each of

With a clean stencil plate, tape off the openings next to the area you will be adding. Align the stencil along the horizontal guide and securely attach the additional portion in place (stencil adhesive works well for this). The extra part of the stencil plate can hang loosely with just a piece of tape keeping it in place, especially if it is covering paint that has not dried hard.

the walls, reality bites. Suddenly, you might find that you have a wall that requires five repeats with an extra three inches, and the next wall will be three inches shorter than that perfect five.

With Chain Link designs, you can often simply run around the room and if it doesn't match, frankly it isn't that big of a deal unless you are a perfectionist or are getting paid to do the job. Or maybe you just want to try your hand at messing around with your design. Keep in mind that when you start to stretch and shorten the design, you need to pay close attention, as this is a perfect opportunity to screw up. Believe me, I know.

When you are dealing with the chain link stencils and you want to make the design fit perfectly on each wall, with the hope you won't have to deal with cramming the poor stencil into a corner, I still recommend you figure out the number of repeats you will have on each wall. This will at least give you an idea of how much you will have to add or subtract to make the design fit.

I can't say which is actually easier, eliminating part of the design or adding extra pieces, as the design will usually dictate that. You may find that you have to do both. Either way, I recommend you do as much of your experimenting on paper first

Other times to make a corner fit, you will need to remove a piece of your stencil design. Again, use your paper samples to help decide the best way to do this.

with either of these options to get yourself familiar with the process. Sometimes if you only need to add or subtract an inch, you can simply offset the registration marks ever so slightly. Often the marks are an eighth of an inch wide; by slightly offsetting the marks, lining them up next to each other rather than on top, you can gain an inch in eight repeats. Of course, it's not always that easy.

In these examples, the same section of the stencil is being used both for eliminating a portion of the design and for stretching the design to fit by adding an extra piece. When you have about two-thirds of the wall stenciled, measure the remaining one-third again and divide it by the repeat length. Use this measurement, and your stencil proof to get

a good idea of what you are going to have to do to make the design fit. You may find it is easier to add one long chunk at the end, or maybe an extra leaf added to each of the last couple repeats would be less work. It will be up to you to make the call on what works best in your situation.

- - - - -

Avoid a Curse (or Cursing)

Stencil damage can easily be repaired, but it is still better to use precautions and prevent damage

Make sure you clean the portion of the stencil that will be overlapping an already painted area to avoid unwanted paint marks. Tape off the area you will be omitting and align your stencil plate on the horizontal guide. Securely attach the portion you will be stenciling and allow the extra stencil plate to hang loosely.

from happening. Never lay stencils on top of each other without some kind of protective layer in between. Bridges can easily catch on one another and rip. Always store a stencil flat, not rolled. If you think you won't have any difficulty unfurling a plastic stencil that has been stored for the last two years in the mailing tube it came in, you are sadly mistaken. When you receive your stencil and are waiting to begin (or when you are finished with your project), lay the stencil in its bag on top of a cabinet (don't forget where you put it) or hang it in the back of a closet from the clips on a pants hanger.

If you are not adding and subtracting bits and

pieces of the stencil design and you have done your paper samples, the chances of making a mistake are slim. One of the most common mistakes you might run into would be to put the wrong color in an area. There is an easy way to avoid this. When you are ready to start your project, do the stencil once again on paper. Now the stencil plate will have a little color on it, allowing you to see what goes where. This is also an asset if you are planning on blending any colors together. Your first pattern will have very true colors since it is a clean plate. If you are blending, your next pattern will likely pick up a little bit of the blending color

- - - - -

Remember, some variation is very acceptable and you can regulate this simply by keeping an eye on things as you move along.

- - - - -

from the plate and it may ever so slightly alter it. So if you do not take this initial step, your first flower pattern on the wall may show the yellow brighter than the rest of the patterns where the yellow picks up a hint of the red you are blending into it. You can wipe off any residue each time you start another repeat, but since the color is usually being altered so slightly, I find this is just more work. Do the initial stencil on paper before you start; it's easier and it's handy; and you can use this sample as a guide when you begin.

The other mistake you may encounter is getting one area darker than the rest of the stencil. Remember, some variation is very acceptable and you can regulate this simply by keeping an eye on things as you move along. Once you start getting some buildup on the stencil plate, it can be misleading. The paint will appear lighter than it actually is when you look at what was just applied through the shadowy outlines of a paint-laden stencil plate. This is an optical illusion and that is why it is important to sneak a peek under the plate to see how things really look. This is especially true whenever you return from a break in your project and start working on it again. You can't just put on the headphones and crank up the music while you aimlessly stencil the entire wall without ever looking at what you have previously done.

Perhaps in spite of my recommendation, you did crank up the music, went off into your own little stencil world and now you notice the last stencil

you did is definitely darker. Here are your options. Depending on how dark it is, you can try carefully repositioning the stencil plate on either side of the darker area and intentionally make each of these patterns slightly darker. This creates a softer transition between the lighter and darker stenciling, giving it the appearance of a variation rather than a goof. But this may not always work.

With oils, you can take a rag or paper towel and attempt to remove as much of the paint as possible through the stencil openings while the stencil is in place. You won't get it all but you might be able to improve on it.

As a last resort, you can use some paint thinner and actually wipe the stencil off the wall. Unfortunately, this does occasionally happen; sometimes the thinner isn't capable of removing the mistaken stencil entirely, and some colors may stain the wall. If this happens, it's time for a touch up. If you need to remove water-based paint from the wall, use a damp rag, which may or may not work sufficiently. You can also use some alcohol, but be cautious with that for it may cause problems with the latex underneath. Remember that unless you are messing around with eliminating parts or stretching your stencil design to fit in a certain area, you are probably not going to have to totally wipe off a stencil pattern, let alone paint over it. It's a worst-case scenario; try other options first. But it still is just a coat of paint and not worth having a nervous breakdown over.

To clean the oil paints from your stencil, wrap your finger in a paper towel and use it to follow the delicate bridges, removing the paint as you go. Pay attention to any tabs or wings that might be easy to catch as well.

Scrub-a-Dub-Dub Will Make You Sad-a-Dad-Dad

As you stand back and examine your lovely stenciling, you might be thinking you'll just throw everything away, so why bother cleaning it up? Certainly that is your choice. But you probably paid good money for the tools you worked with and down the road you might want to stencil

a pillow to match the wall stenciling you just did in the living room. It only takes a few minutes and doesn't cost you much of anything except a little time.

Whenever you clean a stencil plate, you risk the possibility of damaging it. As you hurry to clean off the plate, it is easy to catch a bridge and crease it, or worse—rip it. So be gentle with the stencil; it doesn't take any more effort really than hectically rubbing a rag randomly across it. With oils, simply start off with a clean paper towel. Since the oils do not want to bond to the stencil plate, most of the paint residue will come off quite easily with a dry paper towel. Wrap your finger in the towel and use it to follow the delicate bridges, removing the paint as you go. Pay attention to any tabs or wings that might be easy to catch as well.

You will probably notice a shadowy outline of paint that doesn't want to come off as easily. This won't really hurt the stencil, but since I recommend you take the adhesive off the back at this time as well, get out the paint thinner or mineral spirits and put a little on a clean paper towel. This will easily remove any oil paint left on the front of the stencil. Again be watchful of the bridges and tabs.

Removing the adhesive from the back of the stencil is a little stickier (no pun intended). This will require more thinner or spirits than used for the front and definitely more paper towels. You may want to do this out in the garage or on the sidewalk where it will be less stinky, for you will want to saturate the paper towel to make this job easier, As soon as the first paper towel starts to gum up (and it will) spread it out someplace to dry before discarding and get another. Don't scrimp on the towels or the thinner for this and the task will go faster. Make sure you allow the wet paper towels to air out and dry flat before discarding, as they can be combustible while they are wet. Should you need to clean the stencil this meticulously during your project, make sure it is wiped down and dry before you resume stenciling.

Cleaning acrylic paint off the stencil plate is more challenging unless you have been attempting to keep it fairly clean as you work. Many folks will end up tossing a stencil that ends up with a lot of paint buildup, rather than battle with cleaning it. Supposedly there are some products on the market that make removing the dried water-based paint easier once it has bonded, but I haven't run across anything that works miracles. As long as the edges of the stencil openings still remain fairly crisp, you can keep the stencil and most likely reuse it if you want; but if the image is losing the sharpness around the openings due to severe paint buildup, you too may not find the headache of trying to clean it worthwhile. Consider keeping one

of your lovely paper samples should you need the pattern again. Or if you have developed some sentimental attachment to it, tuck it away. You can always toss it when you run across the crispy critter rolled up in some box under the stairway next to the half-filled gallon of paint that is also too far gone to save.

- - - - -

What a Stencil Doctor Might Do

It happens. Of course it was an accident. You wouldn't deliberately rip the stencil apart now, would you? But rip it did, and now it is flapping around like a loose sail, and that just won't do. You don't need a medical degree in stenciling in order to bring it back to life. Actually, it's quite easy.

First you need to clean both sides of the tear well. You don't have to remove the adhesive off the back either if you have been using it, but do lay the stencil out on some clean paper and rub down the front as best you can. This will also help remove any paint residue from the back if it exists. Grab some clear tape and cut two little pieces— one for front, one for back—that will be a little larger than the rip. Realign the broken bridge and place the tape over it, rubbing it down securely. Don't worry about the overlap of tape in the openings at the moment. Repeat with the tape on the backside. Then take a utility knife or razor blade and gently cut out the excess tape that is exposed in the stencil opening. These repairs are susceptible to breaking again, so be aware of them and stencil gently around the area to avoid repeating this process over and over.

Sometimes you catch a tab or wing and it bends forward, creasing in the process and refusing to lie back down again. Try this simple solution: Grab the tab with the tip of your finger from behind and bend it in the opposite direction

To repair a stencil plate, first clean the stencil as best you can. Cut two little pieces of tape that are a little larger than the rip—one for front and one for back. Realign the broken bridge and place the tape over it on the front side, rubbing it down securely. Don't worry about the overlap of tape in the openings. Repeat with the tape on the backside of the stencil.

Take a utility knife or razor blade and gently cut out the excess tape that is exposed in the stencil opening. The stencil is ready to use again, but be careful as the repair is susceptible to breaking again. Gently stencil this area to avoid repeated repairs.

of the crease. You would be amazed at how easy this works, unless you keep catching and bending it over and over. The first time this happens, try spot spraying a little more of the adhesive on the back to help keep it down, and also make a mental note that you need to be a little cautious in this area while stenciling. Once you damage a stencil, it becomes increasingly easier to do it again. By realizing the vulnerable areas of your design, you can easily continue stenciling without further problems simply by altering your technique, such as not rubbing your brush against the grain.

Stenciling is an easy and fun way to add your personality to your home. You can use as little or as much of it as you want; I have seen original Arts and Crafts homes that have every room in the house stenciled. Even a simple table runner can be a delightful and rewarding addition to a room or a thoughtful gift for someone, especially when you start working with the oils and see how unique and beautiful stenciling can be. So take care of your investment and buy quality items to start with.

I have one final caution for you, so beware! Stenciling can be addicting. Once you get started, you may be hooked for life. ■

A Bakers' Dozen:
Frequently Asked Questions
About Stenciling

1. I have never stenciled before; is it difficult?

Stenciling is really quite simple. Just like everything else, the right tools for the job will make the project easier. Practicing on paper not only helps you become familiar with techniques but also allows you to experiment with colors. They also provide you with handy visuals that you can tape or pin up on your wall or curtains; this allows you to easily make adjustments before you start your project.

2. What are Paintstiks?

Paintstiks are an oil-based paint in a solid form. Just because they are "sticks" does not mean you use them like a crayon. Rather they are a paint medium used with a stencil brush for stenciling. They go a long way, and in most situations you will be lucky to go through even half of one stick of each color you are using in your project. See page 53 for more instructions on their use.

3. Do I need a special brush for stenciling?

Stencil brushes are specifically made with flat end bristles that should be held perpendicular to the stencil plate while painting. This prevents the paint from sliding under the stencil bridges. You will need a separate brush for each color used in your chosen stencil design. See page 58 for more information on brushes.

4. How does the stencil attach to the surface I want to work on?

Although many people may be familiar with using masking tape to hold a stencil in place, repositionable stencil adhesive is by far the easiest way to get your stencil to stay where you want it. It also helps hold all the bridge work down, therefore helping to eliminate paint seeping under the stencil plate and appearing messy. Recoating is only necessary when the stencil begins to loose its tack. See page 60 for more information on stencil adhesive.

5. How durable are the stencils, and do I need to buy more than one of a design?

Today's stencils are cut out of flexible durable plastic and will last for a very long time if taken care of. Unlike acrylic paints that can build up on the stencil plate and distort the edges of the design, oil-based paints do not bond with the plastic stencil plate; so when you are using this form of medium, one stencil should be enough to complete the job. If you are using a water-based paint or if you have a larger job where you plan on mirroring your stencil image, a second stencil may be a worthwhile convenience. See page 31 for more information on stencils.

6. Can I use Paintstiks or other oil stencil paints on latex walls?

Most definitely! More important is the sheen of the wall paint. Flat finishes will dry the quickest and provide the most vibrant colors whereas semiglosses provide problems because the surface is not porous enough for the stencil paint to adhere to. Eggshell and satin finishes stencil well but may take a little longer to dry, and colors may be a bit lighter. See page 87 for more information on surfaces to stencil.

7. Can textured walls be stenciled?

Textured walls stencil surprisingly well. The texture will add some depth to the design and sometimes give it an "old world" appearance. Start with very little paint on the brush and a light touch, adding more paint if necessary. Don't worry about getting the edges of the stencil painted perfectly for when you get five or six feet away, your eye will naturally fill in the imperfections in the outline of the design. If you have a similar texture in a closet, do a sample there to get a feel for it. See page 88 for more information regarding textured surfaces.

8. How do I deal with the corners?

With certain designs the easiest thing to do is to start in the least conspicuous corner and let the corner designs fall where they may. If the starting corner doesn't match perfectly, so what; if it was wallpaper it wouldn't match either. To avoid cramming a stencil into a difficult corner, try this instead: Run vertical pieces of 1/2-inch masking tape in the corners on each wall. Stencil up and on to the tape, bend the stencil around the corner and continue on. When you pull the masking tape off, you will have crisp sharp edges in the corners, similar to a picture frame mat, and since each corner is done the same, it looks finished and appropriate. See pages 83 and 114 for more instructions on corners.

9. Can I stencil on fabrics as well?

Most fabric stencils beautifully. A nice advantage of the oil-base paints is that they dry to a soft flexible finish, unlike most acrylic-based textile paints. They also blend and shade better. Prewash before and heat-set after as with any painted fabric, and wash delicately rather than dry clean, as the solvents used in the process can dissolve the paint. See page 91 for more information on fabrics.

10. Can I stencil furniture or wood?

Furniture and wood certainly may be stenciled, but surfaces that may be subjected to abuse should be topcoated with some kind of protective finish. Aerosol topcoats work well because they "set" the paint. Low-sheen finishes like flat will allow the most intense stencil colors, whereas higher gloss surfaces will need to be adjusted because paint won't adhere to a nonporous area as well. A scrap of wood on which you can do a sample of the whole process beforehand can be very beneficial. See page 98 for more information.

11. Do I need paint thinner for cleanup?

When you use The Masters Brush Cleaner & Preserver, which is a nontoxic product similar in use to shaving soap, brushes can be cleaned with water even after using the oil-based Paintstiks. Clean stencil plates with a dry rag or paper towel. The only time you need paint thinner for cleaning is upon completion of the job before the stencil is stored. Use paper towels moistened with thinner to wipe off any paint residue on the front of the stencil and to remove the adhesive from the back. See page 61 for more instructions on using thinner.

12. What happens if I make a mistake?

It is best to try to avoid mistakes, but sometimes they happen. Having some variation in the stenciling makes it look hand-painted, so a a little darker or lighter spot can be fine. Paper samples eliminate a lot of potential mistakes, but in a worst-case scenario, wipe the stencil off the wall with paint thinner and try it again after the thinner has dried. See page 117 for more information regarding mistakes.

13. So I need to get rid of it—now what?

So the new homeowners want yellow instead of green? Just prime the stencil design and repaint. It's that simple and so much easier than stripping wallpaper.

Glossary

ACRYLIC PAINT – A water-based paint where the pigment (color) uses a synthetic binder mixed with water to make the color stick to the surface. Acrylic paints generally dry quickly and clean up with water, but can be quite messy to stencil with.

ADHESIVE (REPOSITIONAL) – An aerosol glue that is applied to the back of the stencil plate to create an adhesion that will stick to the surface to be stenciled. The stencil can then be repositioned many times before needing to be recoated.

BRIDGES – Also referred to as "ties," these are the parts of the stencil pattern that connect the larger open areas, holding the stencil together (like an "O"). They also are used to form part of the design (like veins in a leaf).

COLOR WHEEL – A diagram featuring the three primary colors of red, blue and yellow spaced equally apart. Spaces between the primary colors feature combinations of the two colors, thus creating the secondary and tertiary colors.

GUIDELINES – A permanent or temporary guide to keep your pattern running straight. This may be a picture rail, chair railing or other wainscot, or it may be a mark like a chalk line.

HUE – Another name for color. For example, blue is a hue, but there are lots of blues such as navy, royal, and sky blue.

INTENSITY – The brightness or dullness of a color or hue. For example, yellow can have the intensity of a sunny yellow or a duller mustard.

LATEX PAINTS – Latex is a generic term for any water-based paints that use synthetic binders in the paint and can refer to everything from artist and craft paints to the paint on a house.

MEDIUMS – Another word for paint, either oil- or water-based. Pure mediums are colorless.

OIL-BASED PAINTS – Paints that use an oil binder (such as linseed oil) to make the pigment (color) stick to the surface. Oils are easier to work with for shading and blending purposes.

OVERLAY – A second stencil plate used on top of the first stenciled image, usually used to separate colors or add additional details. A single stencil plate is also referred to as a single overlay.

PALETTE – A surface used for mixing or holding paint before transferring it to the stencil.

PRIMARY COLORS – Red, blue and yellow, from which all other colors are born.

REGISTRATION – The vertical guide used to align the stencil with each repeat of the pattern, most often a small triangle or diamond cut out in the corners of the stencil plate. It can also be an adjacent portion of the design that is cut out at either end of the plate and lined up on top of the previously painted portion of the pattern.

REPEAT – A stencil pattern repeating over and over to form a border.

SECONDARY COLORS – Created when two primary colors are mixed. For example, red + yellow = orange.

SHADE – Darkening a color by adding black (opposite of a tint).

STENCIL PLATE – A pattern or design cut out of a material such as plastic or heavy paper stock. When paint is applied on top, the image is transferred through the openings onto a surface, such as a wall or fabric.

STENCIL TYPES

BACKGROUND – (or reverse stenciling) the background of the design is applied instead of the image.

BEADING – a type of Chain Link design that works well both horizontally & vertically

CHAINLINK – the same image is repeated over and over like links of a chain

DOMINANT – a dominant image connected by a less significant image like a bar

OUTLINE – only the outline of the design is stenciled, filling it in afterwards by hand

OVERALL – the pattern is stenciled all over the wall rather than a border or spot of design

PANEL – designs that are easy to adjust in length to fit in paneled areas

SPOT – only a portion or spot of design is applied rather than repeated like a border

TERTIARY COLORS – Created when a secondary color is mixed with a primary color

TINT – Lightening up a color by adding white (opposite of a shade).

VALUE – How light or dark a color is, often thought of along a grayscale line as in a light gray vs. black Different colors also have value, such as yellow having a lighter value than purple.

Resources

Suppliers

AMY MILLER
TRIMBELLE RIVER STUDIO
P. O. BOX 568, Ellsworth, WI 54011
715-273-4844 /715-273-4806 fax
www.trimbelleriver.com
*Precut Arts & Crafts period stencil designs and
stenciling supplies*

SHIVA PAINTSTIKS,
Jack Richeson & Co. Inc.
P. O. Box 160, Kimberly, WI 54136
www.richesonart.com
Shiva Paintstiks® & art supplies

DELTA TECHNICAL COATINGS INC.
www.deltacrafts.com
Crafts supplies, stencil adhesive, crème paints

DARD HUNTER STUDIOS
740-779-3300
www.dardhunter.com
*Stencils and other great Arts & Crafts accessories
for the home*

ANN WALLACE & FRIENDS
PRAIRIE TEXTILES
P. O. Box 2344, Venice, CA 90294
213-617-3310
www.annwallace.com
Finished textiles, stencils, yardage

DIANNE AYRES
ARTS & CRAFTS PERIOD TEXTILES
5427 Telegraph Ave. Ste W2
Oakland, CA 94609
510-654-1645
www.textilestudio.com
Finished textiles, yardage

MARTHA FRANKEL
THISTLE HANDWERKS
P. O. Box 21578, Billings, MT 59104
406-896-9434
www.thistlehandwerks.com
*Textiles influenced by the Scottish Arts & Crafts
Movement*

Sites to Visit for Period Stenciling

**SWEDENBORGIAN
CHURCH OF SAN FRANCISCO**
2107 Lyon St,
San Francisco, CA 94115
415-346-6466

GLENSHEEN MANSION
3300 London Road
Duluth, MN 55804
888-454-GLEN
www.d.umn.edu/glen

EL JEBEL SHRINE
4625 W. 50th Avenue
Denver, CO 80212
303-455-3470
www.eljebelshrine.org

LANTERMAN HOUSE
4420 Encinas Drive
La Canada Flintridge, CA 91011
818-790-1421

HOTEL PATTEE
1112 Willis Ave.
Perry, IA 50220
888-424-4268
www.hotelpattee.com
Request the Gustav Stickley room

PURCELL-CUTTS HOUSE
2328 Lake Place
Minneapolis, MN
888-642-2787 ext. 6323
www.artmia.org

LAKE QUINAULT LODGE
P O Box 7
Quinault, WA 98575
800-562-6672
www.visitlakequinault.com

NATIONAL FARMERS' BANK
101 N. Cedar Street
Owatonna, MN

MABEL TAINTER THEATER
205 Main Street
Menomonie, WI 54751
715-235-9726

AHWAHNEE HOTEL
Yosemite National Park
559-253-5635
www.yosemitepark.com

Arts & Crafts Periodicals

AMERICAN BUNGALOW
123 S Baldwin Ave.
Sierra Madre, CA 91024
626-203-0308
www.ambungalow.com

STYLE 1900
199 George St.,
Lambertville, NJ 08530
609-397-4104
www.style1900.com

ARTS & CRAFTS HOME
108 E Main St.
Gloucester, MA 01930
978-283-3200
www.oldhouseinteriors.com